CONTENTS

Ships in Focus Publications

Correspondence and editorial:
Roy Fenton
18 Durrington Avenue
London SW20 8NT
020 8879 3527
rfenton@rfenton.demon.co.uk

Orders and photographic:
John & Marion Clarkson
18 Franklands, Longton
Preston PR4 5PD
01772 612855
shipsinfocus@btinternet.com

Printed by Amadeus Press Ltd., Cleckheaton,
Yorkshire.
Designed by Hugh Smallwood, John Clarkson
and Roy Fenton.
SHIPS IN FOCUS RECORD
ISBN 978-1-901703-89-4

SUBSCRIPTION RATES FOR RECORD

Readers can start their subscription with
any issue, and are welcome to backdate it to
receive previous issues.

	3 issues	4 issues
UK	£24	£31
Europe (airmail)	£26	£34
Rest of the world (surface mail)	£26	£34
Rest of the world (airmail)	£31	£41

SHIPS IN FOCUS R
July 2009

Apologies to readers who were kept waiting for 'Record' 42, which did not
appear until late in April, due to a combination of circumstances affecting
both editors and our printers. Our aim is to publish 'Record' in March, July
and November each year, although we would prefer not to be tied down to
exactly when in each of these months it comes out. Sometimes a photograph
that we need to complete a feature is slow in turning up, and our preference is
for a modest delay in publication rather than incompleteness.

Although we would not use it as an excuse for our lateness, Ships in
Focus are particularly busy producing books at present. This year we have
already published Graeme Somner's 'Ben Line', which has been praised
for the very high quality of the photographic reproduction achieved by our
friends at Amadeus Press. At the end of May appeared 'Wanganella - Awatea
- Monowai: A Tasman Trio'. Although our hopes are that this will sell well
in Australia and New Zealand, the three ships featured all have very strong
connections with the UK, all being built here and two being ordered by UK
companies. Authors Murray Robinson and Andrew Bell have, in our clearly
biased opinion, produced a text which can serve as an object lesson in writing
the history of individual ships. Needless to say, it is also highly illustrated.

Well on in production is a book on the contribution of coasters to
military operations during the Second World War by John de S. Winser, the
acknowledged expert on wartime merchant ship employment. Following this
will be two books on major British coaster companies and, more distantly,
a fleet history of a major liner company. We would not wish to put exact
publication dates to any of the last three mentioned. Well aware that we are in
the midst of a serious recession, we are striving to reduce our production costs
by laying out the text ourselves and, increasingly, doing our own scanning of
illustrations. This way we can maintain our quality but reduce print runs to
the appropriate levels, given the specialist nature of the market for shipping
books. Maintaining editorial and production standards are our top priorities,
and we would sooner be late than compromise these.

In the editorial to 'Record' 42 we were careful to say that *certain*
museums were guilty of policies that restricted our use of their photographs.
Our criticisms were certainly not aimed at the photographic departments of
several organisations with whom we enjoy excellent relationships, notably
Glasgow University Archives, the National Museum of Wales, the Imperial
War Museum and the National Maritime Museum at Greenwich. At the last
named we particularly value the help of David Hodge and Bob Todd, who both
go to great lengths to be helpful and who also read our output with great care.
John Clarkson   Roy Fenton

July 2009

Malayan Prince was one of two Victory types in the post-war Prince Line fleet.
A further photo and details appear on page 139. *[Roy Fenton collection]*

PRINCE LINE POST-1945:
Round-the-world service and tramping
George Swaine

With the ending of the Second World War, and in common with other shipping companies, Prince Line faced a number of problems in resuming their pre-war trades. At that time, although Prince Line (and their associated company, the Rio Cape Line) shared a ship management structure and officers with the ships of Furness Withy and Johnston Warren, the commercial administration was entirely separate; the 'regimental' sense being reinforced by distinctive paint schemes for ships and funnels as well as differing uniform, cap badges and house flags. The board also shared a number of directors with the parent company, namely the Chairman Ernest Murrant, Frank Charlton and Geoffrey Murrant. Commercial control lay with the Managing Director W. MacGillivray, who was recruited by James Knott in 1909, and two other directors, John Barron and Charles Bulmer, the latter being responsible for the Mediterranean trade. I was interviewed prior to my apprenticeship by Mr MacGillivray and my indentures were signed by Mr Barron.

The heavy losses experienced during the war (14 ships) were to a certain extent compensated for by 12 new buildings accepted during hostilities, although three of these new vessels were to be included in the losses. The war standard ships were of variable quality; some being purpose-built for liner trades and others of a more basic general purpose type, leavened by the acquisition of some US-built Victory-type vessels. The loss by enemy action of two of the four prestigious 'Compass boats' normally employed on the New York - Plate service and five of the six remaining impressive purpose-built round-the-world service cargo

liners (in 1928 *Asiatic Prince* (3) was lost in the Pacific under still unexplained circumstances) was particularly felt.

Another factor was the vastly changed political climate, coupled with the physical ravages of war, especially in the Far East. This meant that once reliable sources of freight in the form of both manufactured goods and raw materials could no longer be depended upon to produce what today would be called an assured revenue stream.

Most of the larger British liner companies, including some in the Furness group, did not face this problem to the same extent. Despite the financial and political eclipse of the British Empire by the United States, the greater part of the still dominant British fleet was organised into freight conferences (commercial groupings of companies regulating freight arrangements in a particular trade), mostly trading to the old dominions and colonies. The illusion of a return to normality was given by the absolute necessity to export large quantities of manufactured goods and return with cargoes to feed and clothe the population of the UK, coupled with the still strong bonds of sentiment between the UK and these countries, as well as the doctrine of Imperial Preference - then extant immediately post war and before the formation the European Common Market.

Prince Line differed markedly in that two of its three major trades were based in the USA and administered from the New York office of Furness Withy. Just prior to the war, more than 15 British-flag Furness Withy vessels were managed in New York. This unique arrangement in

Egyptian Prince (4) was the oldest surviving ship in the Prince Line post-war fleet, having been built at the Furness yard at Haverton Hill-on-Tees in 1922.

She only just figures in the post-war fleet, being sold in 1946 to French owners who renamed her *Lorrain*. She lasted until 1960, latterly owned in Monaco as

Herculis, and was broken up in Toulon. This is a pre-war view; her forecastle bulwarks were later painted grey. *[B. and A. Feilden/J. and M. Clarkson]*

The 'Compass' *Eastern Prince* (4) (top,
pre-war), built in 1929 by Napier and
Miller Ltd. at Glasgow, did not re-enter
company service post war, continuing her
wartime role as a troop ship (middle and
bottom). She was sold to the Ministry of
Transport in 1946, although Prince Line
remained managers. Ironically on the
30th June 1946 she was the last vessel
to leave Haifa at the end of the British
Mandate, another Prince ship *Lancastrian
Prince* (3) having been the first to use the
new port in 1933 (see 'Record' 41). As
Empire Medway, a name given in 1950 to
free her existing name for a new ship, she
arrived at Faslane to be demolished in
November 1952. *[Ships in Focus; Newall
Dunn collection; World Ship Society Ltd/
Roy Fenton collection]*

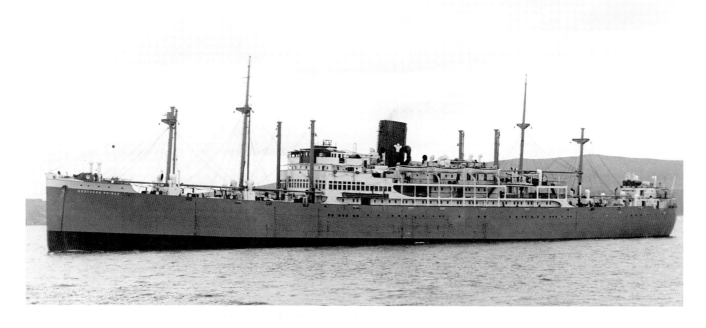

Another ship to see little service post-war was *Southern Prince* (1) (top, pre-war). From 1939 to 1943 this ship acted as a minelayer, being the largest in service (middle). Following the breakout of the German battleship *Bismarck* in May 1941, she laid extensive minefields off the Norwegian coast in case the warship doubled back. In 1944 she acted as headquarters ship for Rear Admiral Rivett-Carnac for Operation Neptune and was then fitted out as a training ship for the British Pacific Fleet. She was not accepted back by Prince Line, being sold to the Government in 1946. She did not enter trooping service and was sold on to Costa Line of Genoa early in 1947, becoming *Anna C* and engaged in their South American service (right). She was broken up in La Spezia in 1972. *[J. and M. Clarkson collection; Imperial War Museum, A 9986; Newall Dunn collection]*

African Prince (4) was completed in September 1939 at Haverton Hill-on-Tees. She lasted with Prince Line until 1961, and was still game for a further career as the Hong Kong-owned *Ardmore* and, from 1965, the *Kali Elpis*. After a long lay up she was broken up at Bombay in 1969. *[Ships in Focus]*

a foreign country was reflected in the size of the Furness commitment in North America, with 18 offices and seven stevedoring and other companies based throughout the USA and Canada. There was also a significant presence in Bermuda and Trinidad and throughout the West Indies, Central and South America through its affiliates and associated companies, Houlder Brothers, Royal Mail Lines and the Pacific Steam Navigation Co.

Origins of the round-the-world service

Examination of James Knott's confidential instructions to masters and agents, sailing lists and other documents dating between 1896 and 1902 fails to reveal any service to and from the USA and the Far East amongst the 16 routes listed (excluding the five tank steamers noted as being owned by the Prince Line (1895) Ltd.). However, by 1908 the company's privately published 'Sailing Directions' go into great detail on

The war-built ships delivered to Prince Line were a somewhat disparate collection, built to several different designs. In post war years they were deployed on a number of different trades and it was not unusual to see them in charterer's colours. All four depicted here had Doxford three-cylinder two-stroke diesels.

Highland Prince (4) came from Burntisland Shipbuilding Co. Ltd. in 1942: note her distinctive bow in this photograph of her leaving Cape Town in March 1952. She was sold to Williamson and Co. of Hong Kong in 1955 and ran as *Inchstuart* until 1969 when scrapped locally. *[John McRoberts/J. and M. Clarkson collection]*

Completed in April 1943, *English Prince* (1) was one of two Doxford motor ships to different designs, unusually having a split superstructure (top). Having spent time chartered out, she was sold to Greek owners in 1961 to become *Simos*. A stranding off Cape St. Vincent in July 1972 effectively ended her career, although she was not scrapped at Bilbao until over a year later. *[Ships in Focus]*

The other wartime building from Burntisland, *Scottish Prince* (4) of 1944 had many superficial differences from *Highland Prince*, both built when standardisation was, supposedly, the watchword in British shipbuilding (middle). Bow, cargo gear and superstructure were treated quite differently, although dimensions were very similar and down below both had the same Doxford engines. *Scottish Prince* was an early sale; in 1952 going under Panama-registry as *Vitali*, but unusually then returning to the British flag for Crest Shipping Ltd. as *Hillcrest*. Further name changes were to *Sophia* in 1959 and *Yannis* in 1966, with demolition at Shanghai following in 1969. *[Newall Dunn collection]*

Welsh Prince (6) of 1944 was an almost exact twin of *Scottish Prince*, which was surprising given that she was built not at Burntisland but by Doxford at Sunderland (bottom). Ownership was first by Rio-Cape Line Ltd. and from 1955 by Furness, Withy and Co. Ltd. 1961 saw her sold to the Vergottis group, for whom she remained under the UK flag as *Vergmont* until scrapped at Whampoa in 1971. *[FotoFlite/J. and C. Clarkson collection]*

ports and coastal passages in Japan, Korea, China, and include comments on seasonal trans-Pacific passages between the US west coast and the Philippines. It is likely therefore that the eastern interests of Prince Line started around 1903/4, initially through expansion of the New York and New Orleans - Brazil and the Plate trade to South and East Africa. This new venture was no doubt given a boost by the necessity to replace revenue lost when the Italian government passed legislation in 1907 excluding Prince Line from the lucrative emigrant trade to the USA by limiting this trade to Italian flag ships. Although trans-Pacific seasonal passages are mentioned, it is noticeable that initially the service had more of a circular nature, outbound cargoes being from New York to South and East Africa with return freights from the Far East, Dutch East Indies, Straits Settlements and India to the US East Coast via the Suez Canal.

The opening of the Panama Canal in August 1914 provided considerable additional potential for the expansion of shipping services, although inevitably there were delays until the end of the First World War. In the interim, James Knott sold Prince Line to Furness, Withy and Co. in 1916 and in the following year the Rio Cape Line (J. Gardiner and Co., Glasgow) was also acquired by Furness Withy and placed under the aegis of Prince Line. (It should be noted that following this latter purchase, a number of ships operated by Prince Line were actually owned by the Rio Cape Line or transferred from one entity to the other as necessary for optimum tax purposes. To avoid complication, this accountancy sub-plot – so typical of the Furness group and other large shipping concerns – is not referred to in this article.) By 1919 the Furness family had in turn been bought out in a management buyout organised by one of the most influential and entrepreneurial men ever to head a shipping company, Frederick Lewis, later Lord Essendon.

Lewis saw the enormous potential of the United States market and was instrumental in the formation and expansion of services such as the Furness Bermuda Line, Furness North Pacific Service and the Furness Red Cross Newfoundland service (acquired from C.T. Bowring in 1929). After the turmoil of the war years and the management buyout, steady expansion was undertaken by Furness Withy under the direction of Lewis. Prince Line's round-the-world service was greatly enhanced by the construction of seven twin-screw 10,000 ton deadweight 15-knot motor ships, of which five were built in Germany and two in the UK. The quality of these vessels enabled the service to be maintained profitably despite the effect of the depression experienced in the 1930s. At the time, a joint service was operated with Silver Line (J. Thompson, Sunderland) but this arrangement did not survive post-1945 changes when Thompsons decided to abandon liner trading.

Two near sister ships were constructed during the later war years to the specification requirements of this trade; *Chinese Prince* (4), yard no. 625, J.L.Thompson and Son, Sunderland in 1943 and *Javanese Prince* (2) yard no. 95, Blythswood Shipbuilding Co. Ltd., Glasgow in 1944. The *Chinese Prince* was fitted with two four-cylinder Doxfords developing a total of 7,800 IHP for a service speed of 15 knots. Changes to the design for the second ship were made at the Admiralty's insistence, resulting in a reduction in length from 490 feet to 482 feet and a small decrease in deadweight capacity. At the time, twin-engined motor ships were thought to be more vulnerable to acoustic mines, so the *Javanese Prince* was completed with a single Doxford engine of 7,725 IHP which gave her the same service speed on a slightly increased (three tons per day) sea consumption; when fuel oil cost around $5 per ton this was not a major consideration.

Chinese Prince (4) shortly after completion and with both 50 ton booms lowered: these were fitted in anticipation of handling heavy artillery, tanks and other items during seaborne assaults. The photographs have been censored by Admiralty, but clearly show measures intended to reduce the distance at which she would be visible. *[Right: Newall Dunn collection, below: Author's collection]*

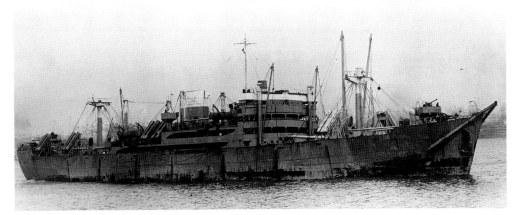

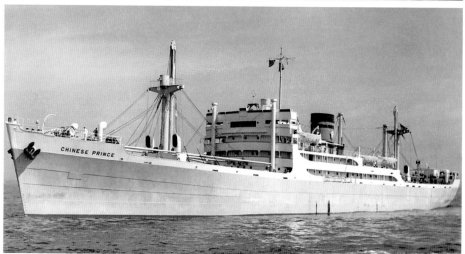

Off Montevideo on 24th August 1947 whilst under control of Furness (Canada) Ltd., *Chinese Prince* still has much wartime equipment, including floats and armour plating across the wheelhouse front (top). Masts are a dark colour and her funnel appears to be all black, but note the beading in anticipation of an, apparently belated, return to peacetime colours.

Around 1948, when *Chinese Prince* (4) was engaged in the New York/round-the-world service, note the wartime signal mast, lookout position on foremast and absence of radar (middle). These matters would be addressed during a regular dry docking period at Taikoo Dockyard, Hong Kong when topmasts and a Decca 159 radar were fitted. Throughout her career she was manned by British officers and Indian deck and engine room ratings, unlike her sisters on this trade which were crewed by British officers, Malayan deck ratings, Chinese engine room ratings and Goanese stewards.

With the delivery of new ships, in 1950 *Chinese Prince* was placed on long term time charter to Shaw, Savill and Albion (not on the bare-boat charter as mentioned in some references), and as the *Nordic* remained engaged in that company's Australasian services for 14 years until her disposal for demolition in 1964 (bottom). *[Ships in Focus; Author's collection; Ships in Focus]*

The Blythswood-built *Javanese Prince* (2) (opposite top) was a near sister to *Chinese Prince* (4) but displayed some differences, including the lack of a poop deck and the treatment of her bridge front. Ownership was different too, at least until 1954 when she was transferred from Rio Cape Line Ltd to Prince Line Ltd., although as explained in the text this made no difference to her deployment. Sold in August 1961 she worked for Ben Line as *Benlarig* until broken up at Hong Kong in 1969. *Javanese Prince* was photographed in South African waters: note the steam tugs. *[Newall Dunn collection]*

By this time, as mentioned above, Furness Withy was established throughout the USA and Canada and well placed to maximise freight revenues. The service settled down to its final form with five ships providing a monthly call at each port. New officers joined in New York, having travelled out on the Furness Warren service's *Newfoundland* or *Nova Scotia* from Liverpool to Boston, or by Cunard Line direct to New York, reporting to Head Office at 34 Whitehall Street – 'where Broadway begins'. There they would be interviewed by the local New York board director, Mr Harris and Furness Withy's redoubtable Chief Marine Superintendent for North America, Captain Sir William Charlton DSC, formerly master of the *Monarch of Bermuda*. New arrivals would then report on board the ship loading at Prince Line's berth, Bush Terminal Brooklyn, operated by Bay Ridge Inc. and owned by Furness Withy. From there could be seen the weekly arrivals and sailings (from Pier 95 North River) of the *Queen of Bermuda* and *Ocean Monarch*, maintaining the well-known Furness Bermuda service.

Officers and cadets had to be prepared for at least 15 months away from the UK, representing three round-the-world voyages each of five months. Such was the popularity of this trade that many opted for a 30-month stint, with some senior officers settling permanently in and around the New York area. A typical voyage schedule would include loading manufactured US goods and military stores in New York, Baltimore, Philadelphia, Norfolk, Charleston or Wilmington, through the Panama Canal to Long Beach and San Francisco then across the Pacific. Twelve passengers were carried and berths were much sought after.

Manila was the first discharge port followed by Hong Kong, three or four ports in Japan, Taikoo Dockyard in Hong Kong for routine hull and engine maintenance, then loading at Manila, Iloilo, Cebu, Tarakan, North Borneo, Surabaya, Djakarta, Singapore, Port Swettenham, Penang, Colombo and then finally to the Malabar coast ports - mainly Cochin where some crew changes were effected. The ship would then head across the Arabian and Red Seas towards the Suez Canal, skirting the Laccadive Islands and Socotra before bunkering at Aden. From the Canal, course would be shaped through the Mediterranean – where the company's smaller Mediterranean service ships would occasionally be sighted – and finally across the Atlantic to Halifax, Boston and New York.

As may be imagined, cargoes carried were many and varied. The Philippines and Indonesia exported palm oil, sugar and manila. At the (then) Malayan ports, rubber, tin and hardwoods were loaded whilst Cochin and the Malabar outports were notable for vast quantities of cashew nuts in season - an absolutely essential part of any sophisticated US East Coast cocktail party at that time. The ships had therefore to be designed to accommodate the resulting extremely complex multiport and commodity stowage together with various vegetable oils and latex carried in a number of specially coated deep tanks.

During the course of these lengthy voyages all manner of weather conditions were experienced. Ever since the unexplained loss of the *Asiatic Prince* (3) north of Hawaii whilst on passage from Los Angeles to Yokohama in March 1928, the ferocity of the tropical revolving storm in all its local manifestations from the West Indian hurricane to the typhoon of the China Seas - so well described by Conrad, Wouk and Montsarrat - was never far from any master's mind during the appropriate season. The fact that the ship was carrying more than two tons of gold at the time of her disappearance has given rise to any number of conspiracy theories but it is likely that she was simply overwhelmed by the gigantic seas that these storms create. All was not gloom though and the company records show that a 90% average sea speed of 15 knots was maintained from 1948 to 1960 on this trade.

In company with the *Chinese Prince*, *Javanese Prince*, *Black Prince* and the sole survivor of the pre-war Far East ships, the *Malayan Prince*, until 1957 Prince Line deployed one of the three Victory ships acquired by the group, the *British Prince* (5), in this trade.

With the delivery of *Eastern Prince* and *Cingalese Prince* for the round-the-world service, opportunity was taken to replace the rather unsuitable 'fast standard' turbine ship, the *Black Prince* (3) ex-*Empire Regent* which was then time chartered as the *Zealandic* to Shaw, Savill and Albion, another Furness subsidiary. She was sold to Canadian Pacific in 1952, becoming the *Beaverlodge,* and in 1960 the *Benhiant* of Ben Line. After carrying the name *Venus* for a year she was scrapped at Kaohsiung in 1971. *[World Ship Society Ltd.]*

Built by Deutsche Werft, Hamburg in 1926, the twin-screw motor ship *Malayan Prince* (1) was the only survivor of seven sister ships built for Prince Line. She was scrapped at Inverkeithing by T.W. Ward Ltd. in 1950. *[J. and M. Clarkson collection; Roy Fenton collection]*

Photographed shortly after purchase in 1948, *British Prince* (5) had been completed in 1945 by the Bethlehem Fairfield yard, Baltimore as the *Stamford Victory* and was almost immediately transferred to the British Ministry of War Transport with Furness Withy acting as managers. From 1948 to 1957, when she was replaced by another Prince Line Victory, *Malayan Prince* (2), the *British Prince* was on the round-the-world service. Thereafter she was on time charter as *Mandagala* to T. and J. Brocklebank for their UK – India trade until sold in 1960. As *Orient Trader*, she caught fire in Toronto in July 1965 and had to be towed out and beached. She was broken up at Valencia in 1966. *British Prince* had a summer deadweight of 10,639 tons on a draft of 28.5 feet. Five holds, arranged with deep tanks, upper and lower 'tween decks and special lockers had a grain capacity of 562,000 cubic feet and just under 2,000 tons of cargo oil could be carried in eight deep tanks. Two Westinghouse single-reduction turbines powered by two Foster Wheeler water tube boilers producing steam at a pressure of 440 psi for 6,000 SHP were geared to a single shaft giving a service speed of 15.5 knots at 100 rpm. Even then, the daily fuel consumption of 50 tons at sea and seven tons in port, whilst more economical than equivalent British-built turbine steamers, did not compare at all well with similar sized motor ships with a daily sea consumption of around 28 tons. *[Prince Line/Author's collection]*

Built as *Tusculum Victory*, Prince Line's second Victory-type, *Malayan Prince* (2) was transferred in 1954 from Furness, Withy and Co. Ltd. for whom she had been running as *Pacific Stronghold*. Following her sale in 1959 she carried five different names, often for just a matter of months: *Wang Knight*, *Marine Carrier*, *Elie V*, *Oceanic Wave* and *Silver Falcon*, before arriving at a Kaohsiung breakers' yard in 1970. *[Roy Fenton collection]*

By 1950, the 1926 *Malayan Prince* (1) was worn out and sold for scrap. Furness Withy had already ordered a new liner in 1949 from Vickers, Armstrong for the New York - Bermuda run (*Ocean Monarch*) and it was decided to stay with the same shipbuilders and order two vessels designed specifically for the Prince Line round-the-world trade. Furness Withy had enjoyed a long connection with Vickers starting in the 1920s when the first of three pairs of intermediate cargo liners for the Johnston Warren Line service from Liverpool to Canada and the USA to be named *Nova Scotia* and *Newfoundland* were built followed by the well known technically advanced turbo electric passenger ships *Monarch of Bermuda* and *Queen of Bermuda* in the early 1930s. Both the former were to be war losses, the *Nova Scotia* in the Indian Ocean in 1942 with the appalling loss of 863 lives. Vickers built their replacements in 1947/48 and followed these with a series of four vessels for the Furness North Pacific service (see 'Record' 15). The *Cingalese Prince* (2) and *Eastern Prince* (5) were developments of the war-built *Javanese Prince* and for some years, until the advent of the US Mariner type vessel, were regarded as one of the finest types of cargo liner design for that service. They were completed in September and October 1950 respectively, just ahead of the *Ocean Monarch* which entered service in March 1951, shortly afterwards being awarded the American Academy of Design Gold Medal for 'outstanding beauty and radical design features'. The naval architect associated with many of these programmes, W.T. Cairns, joined Furness Withy from Vickers and eventually became the group's Chief Naval Architect, head of the Economic Planning Department and a Director of Furness Trinidad. The Vickers' ships epitomised the Furness Withy post-war big ship look which included a considerable sheer and sharply raked bow combined with a low 'midships accommodation structure, using well-defined

'fashion plating' with a quite long low funnel, a contrast to the stove pipe funnel of their Victory ship running mate.

The master's accommodation was situated on the starboard bridge front one deck below the bridge. Four deck officers' and owner's/pilot cabins were in the same block, forward of number 3 hatch. Three two-berth and six single-berth passenger cabins, each with a bathroom, plus a bar and lounge were arranged around number 3 hatch trunk way, opening aft on to the boat deck. At the after end of the boat deck was another accommodation block for four cadets in two-berth cabins (usually known as the 'half deck'). Two single-berth cabins for a doctor and writer as well as a hospital were also incorporated. Despite British registry dispensation that a doctor was not required on ships carrying no more than 12 passengers, Prince Line practice on this US-based trade with very lengthy ocean passages, was to carry a medical professional. Over 70 crew and passengers were carried with three galleys catering for different nationalities (European, Malayan and Indian) situated amidships on the weather deck with the galley chimneys concealed within the main funnel casing.

By the late 1950s the US was showing distinct signs of flag preference for export cargoes to the Far East and, whilst the import trade held up well, Prince Line found margins being increasingly eroded. Occasionally fill-in cargoes of Cuban sugar to US East Coast ports (pre-Castro) were lifted in an attempt to maintain freight revenue at an acceptable level whilst in the main trade voyage intervals were lengthened. However, a decision was reached at the end of 1959 to close the service.

The *Javanese Prince* was sold to Ben Line as the *Benlarig* and the *Eastern Prince* and *Cingalese Prince* were placed on time charter with Shaw Savill as the *Gallic* and *Bardic*. The two sisters were finally sold out of company service in 1964 to Bibby Line and employed

Eastern Prince (5) probably in the late 1950s: note 'midship 'tween deck crew accommodation (above and opposite page top). Built by Vickers at Newcastle-on-Tyne (Yard No 116), the

Eastern Prince was 470 feet 10 inches long and 63 feet in breadth. She had a summer deadweight of 10,515 tons on a draft of 28 feet 9 inches. Five holds were arranged with two forward

of the accommodation and two aft, with number 3 hold and deep tanks amidships, just forward of the engine room space. A total grain capacity of 603,402 cubic feet was available with

a corresponding bale figure of 540,000. The hatches were served by 17 derricks in all; one at 25-tons swl on the foremast at number 2 hatch, four at 10-tons swl (two each at numbers 2 and 4 hatches), with twelve 6-tons swl completing the outfit. Up to 2,300 tons of cargo oil, depending on specific gravity, could be carried in the deep tanks. The ship was powered by a six-cylinder Doxford-type motor built by Vickers. This engine developed 6,800 BHP at 116 rpm for a service speed of 15.25 knots on a consumption of 31 tons and 4 tons at sea and in port respectively. Unlike in many ships of that period, the block aft of number 5 hatch which is well seen in the port quarter view was not used for accommodation but housed the carpenter's workshop, deck stores and a large rice store.

Between 1960 and 1964 *Eastern Prince* was chartered to Shaw Savill as *Bardic* (middle), and after coming off charter was sold to Bibby as *Staffordshire* (bottom). Her career ended in November 1970 when machinery damage during a voyage from Liverpool to Rangoon left her not worth repairing and she was broken up at Whampoa. *[Fotoflite incorporating Skyfotos via Furness Withy/ Author's collection (2); Roy Fenton collection; J. and M. Clarkson collection]*

The Vickers-Armstrong-built *Cingalese Prince* (2) of 1951, when almost new (top). After a charter to Shaw Savill as *Gallic* between 1960 and 1962 (lower left), she resumed the name *Cingalese Prince* until her 1964 sale to Bibby as *Gloucestershire* (lower right). In 1971 she was sold and briefly renamed *Cresco* before being broken up at Whampoa. *[A. Henderson/Author's collection; D. Wright/Ian J. Farquhar collection; Roy Fenton collection]*

in that company's Burmese trade as the *Staffordshire* and *Gloucestershire* until scrapped in the early 1970s.

Tramping trades

Furness Withy had maintained an active presence in the London chartering market based on the Baltic Exchange for many years, mainly through their own chartering department and that of Houlder Brothers. As well as seeking open market employment for company ships not required for the liner trades of the various group companies, additional suitable non-group tonnage would be chartered in to supplement liner sailings at times of peak demand. This part of the company also acted as brokers to a significant number of outside interests as diverse as (for example) the Canadian Transport Company (the shipping arm of MacMillan Bloedel of Vancouver, one of the world's largest forest product producers), Thistle Line (Allan Black) of Sunderland and a considerable number of Soviet bloc country shipping interests in Russia, Czechoslovakia, Roumania and elsewhere. Many of these connections dated from Christopher Furness's and Lord Essendon's initiatives during the earlier part of the 20th century and, together with the group insurance interests on Lloyd's, made this relatively unknown part of Furness Withy an influential part of the City of London shipping community. As a matter of interest, the chartering operations of Furness Withy were formed into a separate company in 1971. Furness Withy (Chartering) has since developed into a significant operator of Panamax bulk carriers; the company is now owned by the German Oetker group and is the only part

of the once enormous Furness organisation to remain active, the parent company having gone into voluntary liquidation in 2005 after 114 years' trading.

From 1945 until 1971, besides being chartered to other group companies on occasions, Prince Line vessels were also employed in many tramping trades. As a typical example of this type of activity, there follows a brief account of a time charter of one of Prince's larger 'non-liner' ships.

In April 1960, the *Western Prince* (2) was berthed in Cammell Laird's Birkenhead yard alongside the *Windsor Castle* completing for the Union-Castle Southampton - Cape Service and HMS *Ajax*, a Leander class frigate. Up to March of that year, the *Western Prince* had been on charter to Shaw Savill as the *Zealandic*. Whilst manoeuvring in Dunkirk, her bows had been badly damaged when the failure of her main engine to respond to an emergency astern order resulted in the ramming of the quay at over six knots. It is probably an apocryphal addition to the story that, during this exciting incident, a stevedores' dockside convenience was totally demolished; whether there was anyone using the facility at the time is not recorded.

On 22nd April orders were received to proceed in ballast towards Key West. Three days later the Master, Captain Stephens, was advised that the ship had been fixed on time charter to the American Charter and Tankship Company of New York, a member of the influential Kulukundis organisation originating from the Greek island of Kassos and well known in New York and London shipping circles. The rate was 22 shillings per ton deadweight per calendar month for eight to ten months' trading. Most of the crew were unaware of the probable voyage period.

On the 6th May the pilot boarded off Galveston and the ship proceeded up the Houston Ship Channel, passing the battlefield of San Jacinto and the preserved dreadnought USS *Texas* en route. The Master was kept busy attempting to satisfy the pilot's curiosity about the nuptials of Princess Margaret and Anthony Armstrong-Jones in Westminster Abbey, an event coinciding with the ship's arrival. Soon the crew had (for most of them) the novel experience of the United States in full vigour before the eroding effects of the Vietnam War and the drug culture tarnished the 'American Dream' Norman Rockwell-atmosphere prevailing at the time and all still rather novel to British eyes, more accustomed to the drab post-war austerity which was slowly coming to an end at home.

Houston was the first of four loading ports with New Orleans, Baltimore and New York following in rapid succession. Three weeks after arriving at Houston, the ship was outbound on 27th May from New York with a total of 7,035 tons of cargo destined for Lattakia, Beirut, Alexandria, Jeddah, Bahrain, Khorramshahr, Khor el Muffata, Basrah, Karachi and Bombay. The cargo consisted of over 60,000 bags of flour and milk powder – 'Uncle Sam's hand outs'- plus cars, trucks, oil rigs, machinery, steel plate, workshops, boats and bulldozers. Space precludes a fuller description of this part of the voyage, but suffice it to say that, whilst at anchor off Kuwait, one of the firemen emerged from the engine room where the temperature was over 160 degrees Fahrenheit near the boiler and promptly died whilst sitting on number 4 hatch next to the cadets. He was sewn up in canvas by the bosun and cadets and placed in the ship's hospital whilst the Master arranged a burial service in the rather neglected Christian cemetery some miles outside Kuwait.

The ship left Bombay at the end of July bound for Portuguese East Africa having been fixed on a voyage charter basis for a full cargo of chrome ore from Beira and Lourenco Marques to Baltimore for account of Bethlehem Steel. A 30-day voyage followed, mainly in heavy weather (including some interesting days skirting the edge of Hurricane Donna) before arrival at Sparrow's Point in the Chesapeake Bay.

This was a time of mounting discontent amongst British ratings and a manifestation of this militancy occurred in Baltimore. Morale was low because of the death in Kuwait, subsequent other injuries and incidents plus a poor standard of catering – most unusual for a Prince Line vessel. Matters came to head when the crew refused to sail unless

Western Prince (2), seen about 1956, was the first in a series of three sisters, or near sisters, built at Harland and Wolff's Govan yard, the others being *Rowanmore* (2) completed for Johnston Warren Line under a tax depreciation allowance scheme, and *Southern Prince* (2). *Rowanmore* had slightly more deadweight due to an increased beam but had a smaller engine and lower service speed.

The two Prince Line ships were 466 feet in length with a beam of 61 feet and had five holds – three forward of the bridge and accommodation and two aft. A service speed of 14 knots on a sea consumption of 26 tons per day was provided by a 5,500 BHP Burmeister & Wain-type, five-cylinder, turbocharged engine by the builders. The grain cubic totalled 570,000 including four deep tanks in number 3 hold. Each tank had a five-ton lid which could only be lowered and raised by rigging a gun tackle on one of the derricks at the after end of the hatch. They were secured by lowering the lid and manoeuvring it carefully into place onto rubber gaskets placed around over 300 permanent screws recessed around the edge of the tank and then secured by bolts. A slight jolt or a collision bending one of the screws was the cause of severe delays and much choice language aimed in the direction of the naval architect responsible for this masterpiece of design.

Sixteen 5- and 10-ton swl derricks were fitted with a 50-ton jumbo at the fore end of number 2 hatch. Steam auxiliaries were also fitted and, during lengthy stays in tropical ports, the steam lines through the accommodation ensured the temperature on board was maintained at near-sauna level. No air conditioning was fitted. The ships carried a much smaller complement than the round-the-world vessels and, although the rather spartan accommodation in the port 'tween deck had been designed for an Indian crew, in fact a British crew was always carried. *[Ships in Focus]*

Western Prince (2) was on charter to Manchester Liners Ltd. for their North Atlantic services between 1960 and 1969 as *Manchester Trader*, and was fully repainted. When the charter ended she reverted to *Western Prince*, but was sold in 1971. Her new owner was a member of the Hadjipateras family who renamed her simply *Mariner*. During a voyage from Havana to Kobe in March 1973 she was abandoned about 500 miles east of Yokohama. *[Ships in Focus]*

Southern Prince (2) (above), a sister of *Western Prince*, was placed on time charter to Shaw Savill and Albion as *Medic* (below) for their UK – Australasia services until the mid-1960s when she operated for Royal Mail and PSNC in their South American trades. Following sale by the Furness Group in 1971 she carried the usually string of names: *Argosy*, *Orient Prosperity*, and *Bitas*, ending her days at a Kaohsiung scrap yard in 1978. *[Ships in Focus; J. and M. Clarkson]*

the Chief Steward was replaced; there was some sympathy for this stand and the Master sacked the Steward. After a day's delay, the ship sailed for New York through the Chesapeake-Delaware Canal to load 255 Ford Falcon cars in Newark, New Jersey for Puerto Cabello, Venezuela. A full cargo of hardwood logs was then loaded in the Gulf of Darien near Panama for discharge near a deserted Second World War shipyard upriver from Mobile, Alabama.

Another voyage to the Middle East was in prospect with grain loading in Mobile, Houston and New Orleans completing with a deck cargo of telegraph poles for the Azores before loading some explosives for Aqaba from Kings Bay, Georgia. Ten of the deck crew deserted in New Orleans, having concluded that the voyage was likely to last more than a year. The petty officers, cadets and mates worked the ship from New Orleans to Georgia, where the miscreants were returned having been flown back from New Orleans at Furness Withy's expense with a fine of $1,000 per man.

The voyage lasted in all about nine months before finally paying off. After some necessary and overdue improvements to her crew accommodation, *Western Prince* spent her final years in company service during the 1960s on charter to Manchester Liners as the *Manchester Trader* on their UK-Canada residual break-bulk service. Manchester Liners were pioneering container services at that time but still required a conventional back up. Along with two other Furness group near-contemporary Cairn Line ships, *Western Prince* provided this service for which she was far better suited.

Tankers

Prince Line had been a pioneer operator of tanker tonnage in the 1890s and returned to this trade along with most companies in the group when they ordered two tankers, *Stuart Prince* and *Tudor Prince* in 1960. Despite the nominal ownership of Prince Line *Tudor Prince*, unlike her sister, had the Furness Withy black hull and no 'feathers on the funnel', although the unique Prince Line bridge front badge remained. These 18,600 deadweight ships remained

on long-term charter to BP from completion until conversion to chemical tankers in the early 1970s. They were initially chartered as *Stolt Stuart* and *Stolt Tudor* and finally sold to Stolt-Neilson in 1973.

The ships were worked remarkably hard. It is interesting to note that one commission of the *Tudor Prince* lasted from April 1967 to August 1968. During that time the ship steamed 112,000 miles, carried 300,000 tons of oil, called at 39 ports all over the world and spent 90% of the time at sea - not a GPS or calculator in sight! The longest sea passage was 30 days from Das Island in the Arabian Gulf to La Plata in the River Plate, where on 6th May 1968 she narrowly missed being involved in a massive explosion on board an adjacent tanker. Many other incidents were experienced including the 1967 Arab-Israeli War, the Vietnam War and Aden immediately following the British withdrawal. BP tended to utilise these ships to service small 'out of the way' ports; consequently the navigating officer got a great deal of use out of his portfolio of 3,500 charts, all constantly updated by hand from 'Notices to Mariners'.

At the beginning of these articles, I ventured the suggestion that, for various reasons, Prince Line was not as well known as other companies, both inside and outside the Furness Group. However, it is evident that from about 1945 to 1970 – the so called Golden Age of Shipping – that there was an extraordinary breadth of experience available to Furness - Prince officers ranging from the 'millionaire ships' of Furness Bermuda through many well-established cargo liner trades to extensive tramping both on dry cargo ships and tankers. This inculcated a flexibility of approach that stood people in good stead whatever their subsequent employment during the radical and revolutionary changes in shipping practice, both ashore and afloat, occurring over the 30 or so years since Prince Line ceased being an active operator.

To paraphrase Conrad, 'they were a good crowd'. After paying off, as was the custom, they went their separate ways. Some went east, some north and some south; but none, so far as I know, went west.

The tanker *Stuart Prince* (5) was built by William Doxford and Sons Ltd., Sunderland in 1960. Her sister *Tudor Prince* followed in 1961. Of the two, only *Stuart Prince* was given Prince Line's funnel and grey hull. *[Fotoflite incorporating Skyfotos/Author's collection]*

Sold in 1973, *Stuart Prince* continued in service as *Stolt Stuart* (right) until 1975. She then becoming *Llaima*, initially under Chilean ownership, and was scrapped at Chittagong in 1982. *[Fotoflite incorporating Skyfotos/J. and M. Clarkson collection]*

The tanker *Tudor Prince* (4) was completed in Furness colours but wore the unusual Prince Line bridge front badge, hitherto exclusively the preserve of Mediterranean ships (above and right). *Tudor Prince* became *Stolt Tudor* in 1973, then *Stolta*, next *Stella Azzurra* and finally plain *Azzurra*. She was broken up at Gadani Beach in 1987. *[Fotoflite incorporating Skyfotos/Author's collection (2)]*

W.N. LINDSAY LTD. OF LEITH
Part 3
Graeme Somner and Douglas J. Lindsay

New ideas

In the late 1970s Douglas J. Lindsay, the co-author of these articles, joined W.N. Lindsay after a 20-year career at sea. Douglas Ormiston retired and new ideas came into the firm. An early experiment with management, attending to the operations of the *Portmarnock* and the *Hoylake* for London interests, gave somewhat mixed results not entirely comfortable for an old-established and deeply respectable firm like W.N. Lindsay. This was not helped by the *Hoylake* being one of those naturally disastrous ships which occur occasionally and cause grief (and even bankruptcy) to everyone who come near her, breaking down and getting into difficulties with great frequency. This first foray into third party management (Hay and Co. and W.N. Lindsay were so close, despite being separate firms, that Hay's ships were regarded as virtually 'in house') was on behalf of London-Greeks trading as Orb Shipping Ltd. who had bareboat chartered the ships from the owners, Usbornes. The London interests did the chartering while W.N. Lindsay looked after crewing, maintenance and operations. An unwillingness to pay their bills by the London interests meant that W.N. Lindsay rapidly became disillusioned with the arrangement and they barely lasted a year. But the *Hoylake* was to come back to haunt Lindsays, as will be seen.

In 1978 Douglas W.N. Lindsay retired. The fleet now comprised just the *Roselyne* (2) which traded profitably and well but a single-ship company always has difficulty covering its commitments and this proved no exception. In the meantime W.N. Lindsay's grain and property interests

were developing strongly and all available capital was being directed that way – the company did not believe in debt. So there was little prospect of the shipping activities being expanded from W.N. Lindsay's internal resources. A brief flirtation with running a liner service to Sullom Voe for the construction industry in 1977/78 with the chartered *Cap Carrier* (689/1971) was profitable while it lasted but did not gain sufficient support from shippers to justify its continuation.

D.J. Lindsay Marine Ltd.

At the beginning of 1979 another prospect arose. The *Roselyne* had been placed on the sale market and a newly-formed firm, Longhaven Quarries, showed an interest in her. As its name suggests, this firm was planning to operate a quarry at Longhaven, just south of Peterhead, and had obtained contracts to supply armour stones and other rock material to the Delta project in Holland. Negotiations led to a deal whereby Longhaven would buy the *Roselyne,* Douglas J. Lindsay would take the remaining trade connections, business and goodwill of W.N. Lindsay (Shipowners) Ltd., and set up his own independent company to manage the *Roselyne* for Longhaven, and would look after the other ships which Longhaven intended to buy.

So D.J. Lindsay Marine Ltd. was established and started trading in June 1979 providing ship management, port agency and brokerage services from a base just down the road from the W.N. Lindsay office in Leith. By the end of the year Longhaven had reached an agreement with

Hoylake, passing Freckleton, on her way up the River Ribble to Preston. *[J. and M. Clarkson]*

Ganton whilst in Usborne's ownership. *[Ships in Focus]*

Usbornes to acquire their ships *Ganton, Turnberry* and *Cypress Point* on advantageous terms. This would have been a good deal except that the *Cypress Point* was the old *Hoylake,* with which ship Lindsay had previous experience. Despite being begged not to buy it, Longhaven went ahead with the deal and the *Cypress Point* proved as disastrous for her new owners as she had been for every other operator unfortunate enough to have any involvement with the ship. There were other problems, too. On 14th December 1979 the *Ganton* stranded at St. Mary's Lighthouse, Whitley Bay, and it took four days to get her off the rocks. Her bottom was completely ripped out and it was a fine judgement whether or not to abandon her as a constructive total loss, but she had been the best of the Usborne ships so a decision was made to repair her. She was rebuilt on the Tyne and sailed once more on 22nd February 1980.

By early 1980 it was also becoming apparent that Longhaven was not as well funded as it purported to be, and the whole enterprise collapsed in late spring. To cover their exposures D.J. Lindsay Marine Ltd. briefly reacquired the *Roselyne* but sold it quickly to realise the value.

Final operations

Tainted by the collapse of Longhaven, D.J. Lindsay Marine Ltd. was wound up shortly afterwards after the briefest of independent existences. But Douglas J. Lindsay formed two other companies: Marlin Shipping Ltd. to provide ship management services, and Lindsay Terminals and Trading Co. Ltd. to provide agency, brokerage, and port facility services, mainly at Leith. Throughout these upheavals management services continued to be provided for the *Shetland Trader* (4), which had come over to D.J. Lindsay Marine Ltd. when it was set up. For a couple of years the small enterprise survived on the Hay connection, and agency and brokerage work, before ship management contracts began to come again.

The first of these was the *Roseland,* ex-*Barney Mac.* She was followed for the same owners by the *Rosemount,* ex-*Pearl,* bought direct from Stephenson

Clarke, and the *Rosehill* ex-*Grimsby,* a Japanese logger type of over 4,000 tonnes deadweight. These ships were operated in deep-sea trades and got as far as India and East Africa. The *Scan Trader 1,* ex-*Nordanvik,* was brought under management in 1982. This ship was a self-discharger with a sophisticated system of conveyor belts and which had previously been owned and operated for Swedish cement interests. She was acquired for an intended traffic with aggregates from North Wales for self-discharging on the Thames but when this failed she was first tramped in the open market, then had the self-discharging gear cut out of her so she could trade as a straightforward bulk carrier. Her nominal owners varied as she moved from Swedish to UK to Panamanian flag, although the interests behind her remained the same throughout. Fitted with a small bow thruster she spent some years trading to Southern Greenland in the summer season before being sold to US interests who kept her going until she was scrapped in 2003. Marlin Shipping's management contract ceased in mid-1984.

Roseland at St. Sampsons, Guernsey. *[D.J. Lindsay collection]*

The self-discharging limestone carrier *Scan Trader 1*. *[J. and M. Clarkson collection]*

Marlin Shipping Ltd. also managed two small tankers, the *Davak,* ex-*Fernhurst,* and the *Osunic 1* ex-*Melina.* These ships were owned by Nigerian interests and intended for the Nigerian bunker trades, but this proved to be a difficult business and, with both ships approaching special survey, they were scrapped in 1984 and 1985 respectively.

By late 1984 the business was in difficulties, the ships not earning profits and their owners struggling. Of the remaining ships under management at this time, the *Shetland Trader* (4) was passed back to her owners, the *Roseland* went to the breakers and the *Rosemount, Rosehill* and *Scan Trader I* went to other owners. At the beginning of 1985 Marlin Shipping Ltd. and Lindsay Terminals and Trading Ltd. closed their doors and that marked the end of Lindsay involvement in shipping.

Captain James Bruce, the firm's leading captain (left). Mother, Mrs. Roberta Lindsay (middle) with Jimmy Thompson, *Roseneath's* first mate, painting the wing of the bridge. Jimmy Herd, second mate, Jimmy Thompson and probably Wilson Cardno, a deckhand and subsequently engineer with the company (right). All are Buckie men. *[D.J. Lindsay collection]*

Managed for the Ministry of War Transport, London

EMPIRE MAYRING 1946
O.N. 180464 395g 124n
144.0 x 27.1 x 8.0 feet
T. 3-cyl. by Amos and Smith Ltd., Hull; 9 knots.
10.8.1945: Launched by Cochrane and Sons Ltd., Selby (Yard No. 1305).
1.1946: Completed for the Ministry of War Transport, London (W.N. Lindsay Ltd., Leith, managers) as EMPIRE MAYRING.
20.3.1946: Owners became Ministry of Transport, London.
1946: Managers became Singapore Straits Steamship Co. Ltd., Singapore.
1947: Sold to Ta Hing Co. (Hong Kong) Ltd. (Mollers Ltd.), Hong Kong and renamed SING HING.
1949: Managers became Wallem Ltd., Hong Kong.
1951: Sold to the Pakistan Steam Navigation Co. Ltd. (A.K. Khan and Co., managers), Chittagong, East Pakistan and renamed ISLAMABAD.
1972: Owners became the Bangladesh Steam Navigation Co. Ltd. (A.K. Khan and Co., managers), Chittagong, Bangladesh.
2006: 'Lloyd's Register' records continued existence in doubt.

Empire Mayring. [Douglas J. Lindsay collection]

Managed by Lindsay Terminals and Trading Co. Ltd. and later Marlin Shipping Ltd., Leith

1. ROSELAND 1983-1984

O.N. 301374 1,143g 550n
228.0 x 35.9 x 15.1 feet
Oil engine 6-cyl. 4SCSA by Mirrlees, Bickerton and Day Ltd., Stockport; 1,050 BHP, 11 knots.
19.12.1960: Launched by Clelands Shipbuilding Co. Ltd., Wallsend-on-Tyne (Yard No. 249).
3.1961: Completed for the Kyle Shipping Co. Ltd. (Monroe Brothers, managers), Liverpool as KYLEBANK.
1970: Managers became Stephenson Clarke Shipping Ltd., London.
1.8.1971: Managers became William Robertson Shipowners Ltd., Glasgow.
1975: Sold to William Robertson Shipowners Ltd., Glasgow and renamed TURQUOISE.
1978: Transferred to Stephenson Clarke Shipping Ltd., London.
20.4.1979: Sold to Estland Maritime Inc., Panama (Shamrock Shipping Co. Ltd., Larne, managers) and renamed ESTLAND.
1982: Sold to Estrella Maritime Inc., Panama (J. Wood, Swanage) (Charles M. Willie and Co. (Shipping) Ltd., Cardiff, managers) and renamed BARNEY MAC.
1983: Acquired by Diplari Shipping Co. S.A., Panama (Lindsay Terminals and Trading Co. Ltd., Leith, managers) and renamed ROSELAND.
3.10.1984: Arrived at Barking Creek, Essex for breaking up by G.W. Tutt. She had been arrested earlier that year.

Kylebank sailing from Preston in 1973. [J. and M. Clarkson]

2. ROSEMOUNT 1983-1984

O.N. 308579 1,598g 1221n
301.8 x 43.9 x 17.0 feet
Oil engine 8-cyl. 4SCSA by Mirrlees National Ltd., Stockport; 1,800 BHP, 11.5 knots.
27.2.1967: Launched by the Goole Shipbuilding and Repairing Co. Ltd., Goole (Yard No. 555).
5.1967: Completed for the Klondyke Shipping Co. Ltd., Hull as SOMERSBYDYKE.
1978: Sold to Stephenson Clarke Shipping Ltd., London.
1979: Renamed PEARL.
1983: Acquired by Bremar Shipping Ltd., Georgetown, Cayman Islands (Marlin Shipping Ltd., Leith) and renamed ROSEMOUNT.

1984: Sold to Iona Shipping Ltd., Cayman Islands (Spenlow Trading Ltd., London, managers) and renamed MULL.
1987: Sold by the Admiralty Marshall to Ocean Carriers Ltd., Colombo, Sri Lanka and renamed GIANNIS.
1991: Sold to Viento del Sur S.A., Panama (J. Mourtos Brothers (Shipping) Co. Ltd., Piraeus, Greece) and renamed ANNA II.
1993: Transferred to Everest Maritime Ltd., Kingston, St. Vincent and the Grenadines (Viento del Sur S.A. (S. and G. Mourtos), Piraeus) and renamed ANNA II.
1994: Sold to Danah Shipping Lines S.A., Panama City and renamed DANAH I under the Belize flag.
30.9.1998: Breaking up began by Khanbai Yusufbhai and Co., Kolkata, India.

Rosemount. [Fotoflite incorporating Skyfotos, 329993]

3. SCAN TRADER I 1983-1984
Self-discharging limestone carrier
O.N. 704616 1,916g 718n
293.1 x 41.2 x 17.8 feet
5.1975: 2,539g 1,730n
319.0 x 41.2 x 17.8 feet
Oil engine 6-cyl. 4SCSA by Maschinenbau
Augsburg-Nurnberg, Augsberg, West
Germany; 2,160 BHP.

9.6.1960: Launched by A/B Ekensburg
Varv., Stockholm, Sweden (Yard No. 223)
as a limestone carrier for Skanska Cement
A/B, Malmo, Sweden as NORDANVIK.
9.1960: Completed.
5.1975: Lengthened and owner's title
became Cementa A/B.
1983: Sold to Circle Shipping Ltd. (Marlin
Shipping Ltd., managers), Leith and

renamed SCAN TRADER I.
11.1984: Sold to Circle Maritime
International (Margeste Ltd., managers),
Panama, converted to general cargo ship
and renamed SCAN TRADER.
1988: Sold to Replica Commercial Inc.,
Panama and renamed SEA TRADER I.
1990: Sold to Montgomery Marshall and
Co., Panama.

Scan Trader 1. [Fotoflite incorporating Skyfotos, 346035]

3.1990: Renamed PATRIC M.
7.1990: Renamed TAUNUS.
8.1990: Sold to Info Link Investment Ltd., Georgetown and renamed MEERA.
1991: Renamed MEERAA and registered in Panama with Mercator Ship Management Inc. as managers.
1993: Sold to Allied Maritime Lines S.A., Panama.
1996: Sold to Allied Projects (Overseas) Ltd., United Arab Emirates and renamed TOPAZ.
3.1996: Sold to Abu Qurra Oil Well Maintenance Establishment, Abu Dhabi, United Arab Emirates, renamed AL-MANJEEL and registered at La Paz, Bolivia.
2003: Sold to Mongolian owners and renamed JASSIM II.
2003: Renamed GULF V.
7.8.2003: Arrived at Mumbai to be broken up.

4. DAVAK 1984 Tanker
O.N. 302570 1,328g 606n
229.8 x 40.4 x 14.1 feet
1971: 1,473g 729n 260.0 x 40.4 x 14.1 feet
Oil engine 6-cyl. 2SCSA by British Polar Engines Ltd., Glasgow; 960 BHP.
20.9.1960: Launched by Blyth Dry Docks and Shipbuilding Co. Ltd., Blyth (Yard No. 378) for Stephenson Clarke Ltd., London as FERNHURST.
2.1961: Completed.
1968: Owners became Stephenson Clarke Shipping Ltd.
1971: Lengthened.
1983: Sold to Osunic International Ltd., Panama and renamed DAVAK.
1984: Managed by Marlin Shipping Ltd., Leith.
1984: Broken up at Lisbon, Portugal.

5. OSUNIC 1 1984 Tanker
485g 260n
203.5 x 30.2 x 12.0 feet
Oil engine 6-cyl. 2SCSA by Ansaldo S.p.A. Stabilimento Meccanico, Genoa, Italy; 1,000 BHP.
19.3.1969: Launched by Cantiere Navali Sporbini, Spezia, Italy for Tankimica d'Armamento, Cagliari, Sardinia as MELINA.
6.1969: Completed.
1980: Sold to Osunic International Ltd., Panama and renamed OSUNIC 1.
1.1984: Managed by Marlin Shipping Ltd., Leith
26.6.1984: Laid up at Rotterdam.
9.1985: Sold by auction, on behalf of the creditors of the owners, for breaking up at Ghent, Belgium.

6. ROSEHILL 1984
2,794g 1,710n 4,587d
94.8 x 14.5 x 6.15 metres
Oil engine 6-cyl. 4SCSA by Hanshin Nainenki Kogyo, Kobe, Japan; 2,500 BHP, 12 knots.
1966: Completed by Ujina Zosensho, Hiroshima, Japan (Yard No. 455) for

Seen in May 1963, the tanker *Fernhurst* was later to become *Davak*. [J. and M. Clarkson]

Yamashita Unyu K.K., Nishiuwa, Ehime, Japan as KYONAN MARU.
1971: Sold to Steelycare Shipping Co. S.A., Panama (Commercial Shipping Corporation S.A. (K. Eliopoulos and A. Panagiotidis), Piraeus, Greece) and renamed STEELY CARRIER under the Greek flag.
1974: Transferred to Aspa Maritime Co. S.A., Panama (Commercial Shipping Corporation S.A. (A. Panayotidis), Piraeus) and renamed ASPA.
1979: Sold to Lion Maritime Inc., Panama and renamed LION.
1980: Sold to Carrie Shipping Co. Ltd., Limassol, Cyprus (Ippocampos Maritime Hellas Ltd., Piraeus) and renamed CARRIE.
1981: Sold to Bilingual Shipping Corporation, Panama (Interorient Navigation Co. Ltd. (W. Schindlmayr), Limassol) and renamed GRIMSBY.
1983: Managers became Maritime Management Ltd., Melton Mowbray, Leicestershire.
1984: Acquired by Diplari Shipping Co.

Ltd., Panama (Marlin Shipping Ltd., Leith, managers) and renamed ROSEHILL
1984: Sold to Royal Navy Carriers Ltd., Panama and renamed CATALINA 1.
17.4.1985: Broken up at Gadani Beach.

Managed for Hay and Company, Lerwick
Hay and Company (Lerwick) Ltd., Lerwick
Hay and Co is an old-established trading company in Shetland which entered ship owning in 1954 after chartering W.N. Lindsay ships since 1946. Lindsay provided management services for all Hay ships from 1954 to 1984.

1. COLUMBINE 1954-1957
O.N. 160294 347g 121n
142.8 x 23.6 x 10.5 feet
T. 3-cyl. by Aitchison, Blair Ltd., Clydebank; 79 NHP.
6.1934: Completed by Scott and Sons, Bowling (Yard No.326) for the Newry and

Grimsby later became *Rosehill* under Lindsay management. [Fotoflite incorporating Skyfotos, 288809]

Columbine was a classic steam coaster, seen here on the Manchester Ship Canal. *[Ken Cunnington]*

Kilkeel Steamship Co. Ltd. (Joseph Fisher and Sons Ltd., manager), Newry as THORN.
1954: Acquired by Hay and Co. (Lerwick) Ltd. (W.N. Lindsay Ltd., Leith, manager), Lerwick and renamed COLUMBINE.
24.12.1957: Ran aground at North Head, Peterhead and broke up in heavy seas, her forepart sinking 30.12.1957. She was on a voyage from Baltasound, Shetland Islands to Middlesbrough with a cargo of serpentine stone.

2. RORA HEAD 1956-1958
O.N. 146147 492g 226n
165.5 x 25.7 x 9.7 feet
T. 3-cyl. by Day, Summers and Co. Ltd., Southampton; 91 NHP.
1959: Oil engine 5-cyl. 2SCSA made in 1941 by Harland and Wolff Ltd., Belfast.
15.10.1921: Launched by Day, Summers and Co. Ltd., Southampton (Yard No.188).
10.1921: Completed for the General Steam Navigation Co. Ltd., London as BLACKCOCK.

10.1937: Sold to the Brook Shipping Co. Ltd. (Comben Longstaffe and Co. Ltd., managers), London and renamed BROOKTOWN.
11.1937: Sold to A.F. Henry and MacGregor Ltd., Leith.
1938: Renamed RORA HEAD.
12.1939: Sold to the North of Scotland and Orkney and Shetland Steam Navigation Co. Ltd., Aberdeen.
7.1956: Acquired by Hay and Co (Lerwick) Ltd., Lerwick (W.N. Lindsay Ltd., Leith, managers).
5.1958: Sold to Gaspare Russo, Trapani, Italy and renamed GASPARE.
1959: Converted to a motor vessel.
24.10.1970: Breaking up began at Trapani.

3. SHETLAND TRADER (1) 1958-1964
O.N. 84367 452g 226n
153.6 x 27.2 x 11.2 feet
Oil engine 4SCSA 6-cyl. by N. V. Werkspoor, Amsterdam; 390 BHP.
8.1948: Completed by Bodeswes Scheeps., Martenshoek (Yard No. 370) for N.V. Motorvrachtschip 'Magna Pete', Rotterdam as MAGNA PETE.
1950: Renamed VROUWEPOLDER.
1958: Acquired by Hay and Co. (Lerwick) Ltd., Lerwick (W.N. Lindsay Ltd., Leith, managers) and renamed SHETLAND TRADER.
1.1964: Sold to Enid Shipping Co. Ltd., Leith and renamed HAWICK.
3.1969: Sold to Thomas Jack and Co. (Shipping) Ltd., Larne and renamed CLOUDBERRY.
1969: Sold to Dem. G. Kallimasias, Piraeus, Greece and renamed MARKELLA II.
1970: Sold to Spyros G. Halaris, Piraeus and renamed GEORGIOS.
1973: Sold to G. Economou, Piraeus and renamed ALOI.

Rora Head inherited her name from the previous owner but one. On 13th April 1957, she was photographed in a colour scheme which, apart from her funnel, was mainly grey. *[Roy Fenton collection]*

Extensive repairs including replacement of much of her shell plating are carried out to the first *Shetland Trader* (above and left). *[D.J. Lindsay collection]*

Shetland Trader (1) was Hays' first motor ship (middle). *[J. and M. Clarkson collection]*

In 1964 *Shetland Trader* (1) was sold to Edinburgh owners as *Hawick* (bottom). Note how the funnel colours incorporate the Scottish saltire. *[World Ship Society Ltd.]*

1975: Sold to Eastern Mediterranean Line Co. Ltd., Piraeus and renamed FRIENDSHIP II.
1976: Sold to Eastern Mediterranean Lines Shipping Enterprises Ltd., Piraeus and renamed ALOE.
1977: Sold to Redj Shipping Co. Ltd., Limassol, Cyprus and renamed SONIA.
1977: Renamed SEA HORSE.
1993: Deleted from 'Lloyd's Register' as existence in doubt.

4. SHETLAND TRADER (2)/ SHETLAND TRADER 1/LERWICK TRADER (1) 1964-1972
O.N.185737 500g 285n
178.2 x 28.6 x 10.3 feet
Oil engine 4SCSA 6-cyl. by D. & J. Boot 'De Industrie', Alphen; 450 BHP.
1957: Completed by D & J. Boot Scheepswerf 'De Vooruitgang', Alphen (Yard No. 1247) for G. Brijder, Kampen, Holland as HENRIETTE B.
1964: Acquired by Hay and Co. (Lerwick) Ltd., Lerwick (W.N. Lindsay Ltd., Leith, managers) and renamed SHETLAND TRADER.
1.1972: Renamed SHETLAND TRADER 1 and later LERWICK TRADER.
2.1972: Sold to William Dennison (Shapinsay) Ltd., Kirkwall and renamed HOXA SOUND
1979: Sold to John F. Wilkinson, Kirkwall.
1979: Sold to Albert de Jesus, Curepe, Trinidad and Tobago and renamed TELEBAR but remaining registered in Kirkwall.
1993: Registered at Kingstown, St Vincent.
2001: Deleted from 'Lloyd's Register' as existence in doubt -.

The second *Shetland Trader* was another, somewhat newer, Dutch motor coaster (top). To free the name for a newer ship, in 1972 she became *Shetland Trader 1* and then the first *Lerwick Trader*, as which she is seen loading barley at Gloucester on 24th November 1972 (middle). *[Real Photographs/Roy Fenton collection; Roy Griffin/D.J. Lindsay collection]*

The Dutch coaster *Tromp*, photographed on 19th June 1968 (below), was to become the third *Shetland Trader* in January 1972. *[J. and M. Clarkson]*

5. SHETLAND TRADER (3)/LERWICK TRADER (2) 1972-1979
O.N. 340537 499g 316n
185.0 x 29.8 x 11.8 feet
Oil engine 4SCSA 6-cyl. by Motorenwerf Mannheim, Mannheim; 750 BHP.
4.1963: Built by Scheeps. v/h de Groot & van Vliet, Slikkerveer (Yard 353) for Reederij 'De Noord', Rotterdam as TROMP.
1.1972: Acquired by Hay and Co. (Lerwick) Ltd., Lerwick (W.N. Lindsay Ltd., Leith, managers) and renamed SHETLAND TRADER.
1979: Renamed LERWICK TRADER.
1979: Managers became D.J. Lindsay Marine Ltd., Leith.
1982: Sold to Nialed Shipping Co. Ltd., Gravesend and renamed NIALED TRADER.
1982: Sold to Filaed Compania Naviera S.A., Panama and renamed TRADER.

1984: Sold to Naviera International S.A., San Lorenzo, Honduras and renamed MARGRID II.
1986: Renamed TRADER III.

1986: Renamed JUNIOR GRANT II.
1988: Renamed MARC I.
1988: Sold to Transpacific Marine S.A., Panama and renamed MAK II.

In similar fashion to her predecessor, in 1979 the third *Shetland Trader* (right) became the second *Lerwick Trader* (middle). [D.J. Lindsay collection; Fotoflite incorporating Skyfotos, 346036]

The fourth, and arguably the least attractive, *Shetland Trader* was this British-built vessel (bottom). Handing her back to Hays in 1984 marked the end of Lindsays' involvement with the Shetland company. [Fotoflite incorporating Skyfotos, 104102]

1989: Sold to Mark International Shipping S.A., Honduras and renamed ROSE I.
1991: Sold to Princess Immela S. de R. Ltd., Honduras and renamed PRINCESS IMMELA.
1992: Renamed SAROSA.
1992: Sold to Tropical Seas S. de R. Ltd., San Lorenzo, Honduras and renamed ANDREWSON.
14.2.2008: Still listed by 'Lloyd's Register'.

6. SHETLAND TRADER (4) 1979-1984
O.N.338789 798g 447n
196.9 x 32.4 x 12.9 feet
Two oil engines each 4SCSA 8-cyl by Lister, Blackstone, Mirlees Marine Ltd, Manchester; 1,320 BHP.
22.11.1971: Launched by J. Bolson and Son Ltd., Poole (Yard No. 573).
1.1972: Completed for Hull Gates Shipping Co. Ltd., Grimsby as PARKESGATE.
1979: Acquired by Hay and Co. (Lerwick) Ltd., Lerwick (W.N. Lindsay Ltd., Leith, managers) and renamed SHETLAND TRADER.
1979: Managers became D.J. Lindsay Marine Ltd., Leith.
1984: Owners took over management.
1987: Company acquired by John Fleming and Co. Ltd., Aberdeen.
5.1997: Sold to Shetland Malta Shipping Co., Valletta, Malta, and renamed SHETLAND TRAMP for operation in the Adriatic.
11.1997: Managed by Anti-Plov Shipping Co. Ltd., Rijeka, Croatia and renamed ARTA.
12.1999: Sold to Honduras Maritime Investments, San Lorenzo, Honduras and renamed MARTA.
2004: Sold to Vital Shipping Co.

(Albmarine Ltd.), Durres, Albania.
5.2008: Sold to Largo Shipping Ltd., Marshall Islands (Success M. & S. Maritime S.A., Piraeus, Greece) under the flag of Sierra Leone.
24.11.2008: Still in service.

Managed for Orb Shipping Ltd., London.

1. PORTMARNOCK 1978-1979
O.N. 303863 881g 384n
203.3 x 35.8 x 14.3 feet
Oil engine 2SCSA 6-cyl. by Sulzer Brothers Ltd., Winterthur, Switzerland; 1,201 BHP, 12.5 knots.
17.7.1962: Launched by Cammell Laid and Co. (Shipbuilders and Engineers) Ltd., Birkenhead (Yard No.1308).
9.1962: Completed for Coast Lines Ltd., Liverpool as WIRRAL COAST.

1970: Owners became Coast Lines (Services) Ltd., Liverpool.
1972: Sold to James Tyrrell Ltd., Arklow, Irish Republic and renamed SHEVRELL.
1973: Sold to Usborne and Sons (London) Ltd. (Buries, Markes Ltd., managers), London and renamed PORTMARNOCK.
1976: Managers became Gillie and Blair Ltd., Newcastle-on-Tyne.
1977: Bareboat charterers and managers became Orb Shipping Co. Ltd., London.
1978: Transferred to Fulpass Ltd. (Usborne and Sons (London) Ltd.) (Gillie and Blair Ltd., Newcastle, managers).
1979: Sold to Khodor Itani, Beirut, Lebanon and renamed NADIA 1.
1981: Sold to Mrs Nadia Hussein Mekkaoui, Beirut, Lebanon.
27.11.1985: Foundered in heavy weather off Lebanon.

Built as *Wirral Coast* (upper), *Portmarnock* was managed for Orb Shipping Ltd., London. She is seen as *Portmarnock* whilst in Usborne's ownership (lower). *[J. and M. Clarkson; Fotoflite incorporating Skyfotos, 346037]*

2. HOYLAKE 1979-1980

O.N. 363435 1,235g 1,760d
69.4 x 11.0 x 5.2 metres
7.1969: 1,521g 2,537d
82.4 x 11.0 x 5.2 metres
Oil engine 4SCSA 6-cyl. by Klockner-
Humboldt Deutz, Koeln, West Germany;
12.5 knots.
6.4.1961: Launched by J. L. Meyer,
Papenberg, West Germany (Yard No
504).
10.6.1961: Completed for D/S Hafnia A/S,
Fredrikshavn, Denmark as BROSUND.
25.5.1962: Sold to Franz Hagen, Hamburg,
West Germany and subsequently renamed
JENNY PORR.
1969: Sold to Peter Dohle, Hamburg and
renamed WARSTADE.
1969: Lengthened.
1971: Transferred to Warstade Shipping
Co. Ltd., Famagusta, Cyprus (Peter Dohle,
Hamburg, manager).
1973: Managers became Peter Dohle
Schiffahrts K.G.
1974: Acquired by Usborne and Sons
(London) Ltd. (Fairway Shipping and
Trading Co. Ltd., managers), London and
renamed HOYLAKE.
1977: Bareboat chartered to Orb Shipping
Ltd., London (W.N. Lindsay Ltd., Leith,
managers) and renamed CYPRESS POINT.
1980: Managers became Gillie and Blair
Ltd., Newcastle-upon-Tyne.
1980: Owners became Cypress Point
Shipping Ltd., St. Lawrence, Jersey (D.J.

Hoylake. [FotoFlite incorporating Skyfotos, 341816]

Lindsay Marine Ltd., Leith, managers).
1981: Sold to Paralos Shipping Co. S.A.,
Piraeus, Greece and renamed MANA under
the Panama flag.
1981: Sold to Emmanouil Saliagiopoulos,
Piraeus and renamed NIKOS under the
Panama flag.
1983: Transferred to the Greek flag.
19.2.1983: Sunk off Cape Matapan in
position 36.25 north by 22.25 east whilst

on a voyage from Chalkis to Algeria with a
cargo of cement.

Managed for Longhaven Shipping (Jersey) Ltd., Jersey and Longhaven Carriers Ltd., Jersey.

Managed by D.J. Lindsay Marine Ltd.,
Leith between June 1979 and September
1980.

Ganton. [FotoFlite incorporating Skyfotos, 338820]

158

1. ROSELYNE (2) 1979-1980
See No. 17 in the Lindsay fleet list.

2. GANTON 1980
O.N.   399g 259n 830d
49.0 x 8.95 x 3.81 metres
Oil engine 4SCSA 6-cyl. by Kloeckner-
Humboldt-Deutz A.G., Koeln, West
Germany; 260 BHP, 9.75 knots.
11.2.1961: Launched by J.J. Sietas
Schiffswerft, Neuenfelde, Hamburg, West
Germany (Yard No. 478).
22.4.1961: Delivered to Vega Reederei
Friedrich Dauber, Hamburg as UWE.
1969: Sold to Hans A. Sabban, Hamburg.
3.1974: Sold to Thornby Grain Ltd.,
London and renamed GANTON.
1975: Sold to Five Star Maritime Ltd.,
London.
1975: Sold to Usborne and Sons (London)
Ltd. (Buries, Markes Ltd., managers),
London.
1976: Managers became Gillie and Blair
Ltd., Newcastle-on-Tyne.
1977: Managers became Orb Shipping Co.
Ltd., London.
1979: Transferred to Ontang Ltd. (Usborne
and Sons (London) Ltd.) (Gillie and Blair
Ltd., Newcastle, managers).
1980: Acquired by Longhaven Shipping
(Jersey) Ltd., St. Lawrence, Jersey (D.J.
Lindsay Marine Ltd., Leith, managers).
9.1980: Management ceased.

1981: Transferred to Longhaven Transport
Ltd., St. Lawrence, Jersey (Curnow
Shipping Ltd., Porthleven, managers) and
renamed BUCHANHAVEN
1982: Sold to Grenar Compania Naviera
S.A., Panama and renamed GRENAR
1974: Sold to Karoli Ltd., Valetta, Malta
and renamed KAROLI.
1986: Sold to Kim Shipping Ltd., Valetta
and renamed KIM
1990: Sold to Sress Nidal Beani, Abdul
Ghani Sillo and Tarek Bayazid, Tripoli,
Lebanon and renamed ASSEM.
4.1993: Sold to George Fersen Bahi, Piraeus
and renamed FIRAS R.
5.1996: Transferred to the Honduras flag.
2000: Sold to unknown owners and
renamed NASSER under the Sao Tome flag.
18.7.2008: Still listed by 'Lloyd's Register'.

3. TURNBERRY 1980
O.N. 358743 461g 306n 600d
52.94 x 8.21 x 4.03 metres.
Oil engine 8-cyl. 4SCSA by Kloeckner-
Humboldt-Deutz A.G., Koln, West
Germany.
1.1966: Completed by S.A. Brugeoise
d'Arrimage et de Reparations de Navires
(SABARN), Bruges, Belgium (Yard
No. C42) for Armament Schelderupel
S.A. (Roger Adrien-P Leysen, manager)
Brussels, Belgium as ROODEBEEK.
1969: Sold to Reederei Flint & Co.,

Hamburg, Germany and renamed
LISELOTTE FLINT.
1972: Sold to Usborne and Son (London)
Ltd., London (G.T. Gillie and Blair Ltd.,
Newcastle-on-Tyne, managers) and renamed
TURNBERRY.
1980: Manager became Union Transport
(London) Ltd., Deptford.
1980: Acquired by Longhaven Shipping
(Jersey) Ltd., St. Lawrence, Jersey (D.J.
Lindsay Marine Ltd., Leith, managers).
1980: Transferred to Longhaven Carriers
Ltd., Jersey (Curnow Shipping Ltd.,
Porthleven, managers).
1982: Sold to North Sea Shipping and
Trading Co. S.A., Emmeloord, Netherlands,
renamed STERN and registered in Panama.
1985: Manager became Libra Shipping
B.V., Rotterdam, Netherlands.
1986: Renamed SEA EAGLE and
registered in Kingstown, St. Vincent and the
Grenadines.
1991: Sold to Astrid Shipping and Trading
Inc. (France Marine Service, Toulon,
France, managers) renamed ASTRID and
registered in Kingstown, St. Vincent and the
Grenadines.
1992: Sold to Sea River Shipping Ltd.,
renamed CAMARGUE and registered in
Kingstown, St. Vincent and the Grenadines.
1998: Deleted from 'Lloyd's Register' as
existence in doubt.

Turnberry. [Fotoflite incorporating Skyfotos, 270783/D.J. Lindsay collection]

RECORD REVIEWS

CAERNARFONSHIRE SAIL

By Owen F.G. Kilgour
A5 softback, 206 pages,
published by Gwasg Carreg
Gwalch, Llanrwst, Wales,
2008 at £9.50

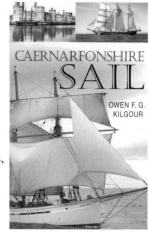

Welsh maritime writers and institutions have been prolific in recording the history of sail in their country – more so, perhaps, than in any other part of the United Kingdom. These studies invariably concern themselves with the ships, seamen, ship owners and trades of the Welsh counties, ports and harbours. No doubt this is what the reader would expect of Owen Kilgour's book, to judge by its title – a title which this reviewer found somewhat misleading.

'Caernarfonshire Sail' is primarily a description of the evolution of sailing-ship types from the earliest watercraft to the four-masted barques of the late nineteenth and early twentieth centuries. The story ranges from log rafts, bark canoes, skin vessels, dugouts and simple plank-built craft, through Scandinavian clinker-built vessels, cogs, caravels, carracks and galleons, to the more familiar rigs of later times: sloops, smacks, cutters, 'one-and-a-half masters' (a term not previously encountered by this reviewer but here embracing galliots, ketches, dandy smacks, yawls, flats and luggers), fore-and-aft and topsail schooners, and square riggers from brigantines and brigs to barquentines, barques and full-rigged ships. Each type is described, often in detail, in terms of its dimensions, hull construction, masting, rigging and sails, with the help of drawings.

The book concludes with a substantial appeal for the provision of a sail training ship for Wales (the author is a founder member of the Jubilee Sailing Trust and its honorary regional organiser for north Wales). Besides its proven human benefits, such a vessel might find a role as part of the contemporary search for renewable energy sources and applications. The construction skills and facilities exist in Wales, finance could be made available, and the vessel would bring together existing Welsh institutions, organisations and activities.

The text is complemented by a useful 13-page glossary of terms used in ship building, hull form, masting, rigging and ship handling; 63 line drawings and 85 photographic plates; and a bibliography of almost 100 references in Welsh and English.

For this reviewer 'Caernarfonshire Sail' ends up as something of a puzzle. What is it trying to say and for whom is it intended? More than anything, it might be described as a guide to the different types of sailing vessels and their purposes; but space would not accommodate mention of all the standard authoritative texts which have been written on sailing-ship construction, rigs and rigging, to go no further back than the nineteenth century. Perhaps it is intended as an introductory handbook for those coming to the subject for the first time and wishing to understand the nature of the craft built in, and trading to, Caernarfonshire, together with something of the economic environment of their times.

Efforts are made to link this catalogue of vessel types to the county and to North Wales generally, although this is not easy in the case of earlier craft such as caravels, carracks and galleons, so that the author has to allude to examples as geographically far afield as Hull, the Thames, the Shetlands, Bremen and Scandinavia. The task becomes easier when we reach 'modern' rigs, since reliable records and statistics are available; but the information provided is restricted to brief generalities such as the number of vessels built in, or registered in, particular ports. There are some attempts to connect older craft to modern examples (e.g., the mediaeval cog to 1950s sailing and rowing dinghies) and to illustrate building techniques (such as the carvel planking of caravels and carracks) by present-day boat building in Caernarfonshire.

The bibliographical references are limited to author and title, omitting publisher, place and date of publication. Some of the titles appear to have little relevance to the book's avowed purpose (Chapelle's 'History of American Sailing Ships', Lubbock's 'Round the Horn before the Mast', Shewan's 'Great Days of Sail', and Time Life Books' 'The Pirates', 'The Pacific Navigators' and 'The Explorers') so that one is tempted to conclude that the list relates rather to the author's wide reading and personal collection.

The unusual composition of 'Caernarfonshire Sail' perhaps reflects the author's special enthusiasms and interests in sailing, boat building and ship modelling rather than the focus which the title suggests.

John Naylon

RAILWAY SHIPS AT WAR

By A.J. Mullay
22 x 28cms hardback,
128 pages, published by
Pendragon Publishing, York,
2008 at £25.00

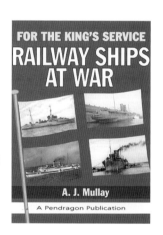

The activities of the railway-owned ships in the First and Second World Wars is a subject of considerable maritime importance and of very special fascination: this book covers not only the passenger and cargo cross-Channel steamers but also those smaller vessels employed in coastal waters, in particular the Clyde and Solent. In setting out a highly readable generalisation of the wartime employment of the ships concerned, the book is likely to appeal to railway enthusiasts seeking an introduction to the wartime marine aspects of the railway companies, the many notable achievements and the regrettable set-backs. Those hoping for a detailed in-depth examination of the ships' service histories may conclude that the opportunity has not been taken to produce the definitive reference book encompassing the detailed story of the entire railway fleet in both world wars. Although printed on high-gloss paper, this hardback publication suffers from certain inadequacies in proof-checking and knowledgeable observers will be surprised by the inclusion of photographs of non-railway ships on the outside front cover, on which black and white photographs have unfortunately been enhanced by the addition of incorrect colour schemes.

John de S. Winser

COAST TO COAST: THE GREAT AUSTRALIAN COASTAL LINERS.
By Peter Plowman
A4 softback. 186 pages.
Published by Rosenberg.
Sydney, Australia at £12.99.

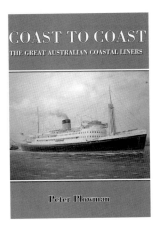

Linking the state capitals of Australia by sea is a fascinating story. In this well-illustrated book Peter Plowman sets out the histories of the ships that did it between Adelaide Steamship's *Adelaide* (1,711/1883) and the same company's *Manoora* (10,856/1036) in 1961. This is the second time that Peter Plowman has written this history for, in 1981, his two-volume 'Passenger Ships of Australia and New Zealand' was published by Conway Maritime in the UK. The format of the earlier books was usually a chapter for each of 201 ships. The new book reiterates much of the material in earlier volumes and unfortunately repeats some of their errors: for example, lavish though A.U.S.N.'s Denny-built *Indarra* (9,735/1912) was, the swimming pool was not an open air one - it was on the port side at Number 2 Orlop Deck level located deep in the ship's hull. Is this an example of a lack of research? A notable improvement is the range of photos and the quality of their reproduction: colour is included where it survives. Excluded from the new book are all mention of Union Steam Ship of New Zealand, Burns Philp and New Zealand Shipping Company. If the reader seeks dates of ship's movements the new book is replete with them for it is a catalogue of the featured ships and almost completely avoids any background information on the trades they served, the cargoes they carried and the extent of competition from Australia's railways and, subsequently, airlines.

Andrew Bell

TRIDENT TANKERS LTD: A CHANGE OF COURSE
By Michael Langley
Quarto hardback. 112 pages.
Published by Middleton Press at £16.95.

The author admits in his preface that this book is something of a hybrid, describing it as blending ship-type evolution and company history. In fact, it also incorporates some personal reminiscences; a three-way hybdridisation that is very difficult to pull off.

The book's title is misleading. Used only from 1962 to 1971, Trident Tankers Ltd. was just one, and by no means the first, name under which the P&O Group

carried out bulk shipping operations. Quite rightly, the book follows these operations from their inception in 1955 through to their demise in 2003, and a much more accurate title would simply have been 'P&O Bulk Shipping'. The impression from this elementary mistake that neither author nor publisher has thought very clearly about the content of the book is reinforced on reading it. An introduction purports to give a history of the tanker, but is brief and very selective in its coverage. The other important ship types which fall within the book's ambit – LNG, LPG, chemical and products tankers, OBOs, ore/oil ships and pure bulkers – have to make do with two-or three sentence descriptions, which are neither satisfying nor definitive.

The bulk of the book consists of lengthy captions to 122 photographs covering most of the ships which have been operated by the various bulk shipping arms of P&O. Oddly, the passenger ship *Dwarka*, several reefers and cargo liners are given this treatment, apparently because they were for a period managed by the same division that looked after the bulk carrying fleet. The captions and photographs are arranged chronologically in six sections, each prefaced with a note about the organisation of bulk shipping operations within P&O during the period. Some captions give an insight into the ship's design, its employment, its capabilities and sometimes even its shortcomings, clearly based on personal experiences and these are particularly valuable. The captions then quickly get into technical details, with not just tonnages and dimensions but engine types and output, descriptions of pumping arrangements and cargo gear. Although a date sold out of the fleet is usually given, no attempt has been made to follow the ship's subsequent career. Interestingly, the very brief bibliography does not mention the major book on P&O's fleet, Rabson and O'Donoghue's excellent 'P&O: A Fleet History' of 1988, suggesting that research has not been that diligent.

The photographs are well reproduced on good quality paper, and range from the competent – comprising black and white and colour aerial views from Fotoflite plus some from P&O's archives – to efforts by the author. Some of the latter are good, and the author often makes interesting comments based on what is visible, but too many photographs are poorly lit or show just a part of the ship, often a view from the bridge or from the dockside. Interspersed with the photographs are coloured cargo stowage plans or diagrams of pumping arrangements. These too are instructive, but the latter at least require more of an explanation for a non-technical readership.

Middleton Press tend to concentrate on rail and road transport subjects, and this may well be their first shipping company history. Certainly, it suffers from a lack of clear direction, consistency and editing. The author has some interesting things to say, and the book is by no means without merit. Yet it falls firmly between three stools, not being a satisfactory history of P&O's bulk shipping operations, not fully explaining the design and operation of the ship, and not doing justice to the author's obvious considerable experience on types of ships which are extremely important today.

Roy Fenton

LIBERTY SHIPS ON CHARTER TO BRITAIN
Part 2: Ships sunk or damaged
John de S. Winser

On the basis of the estimated loss rates approved by the British Combined Chiefs of Staff in August 1943, 17 of the projected 200 Liberty ships were expected to become war losses. In fact only 11 had been sunk by the time the Second World War ended in August 1945; three others had been so seriously damaged they saw no further service under the Red Ensign and, for war and marine reasons, another eight vessels required more than two months' repairs, one of them twice. After the war and while still on charter from the US, one vessel was badly damaged by fire and three were lost. Details of these and associated incidents are given below in chronological order.

4th October 1943: *Samwater* and *Samite*

Samwater was off Cape Tenes (Algeria), on passage from Baltimore to Port Said, when eight German aircraft were sighted at 18.45 and her gunners were the first in the convoy (UGS 18) to open fire, damaging one attacker and bringing down another, which exploded on the vessel's port beam. In the same convoy 25 minutes later, her sister ship *Samite*, carrying 6,732 tons of general cargo from Baltimore to Alexandria, was in position 36.42 north by 01.10 east when a glider bomb hit her port side just forward of the bridge. The violence of the explosion killed one seaman, started a fire in number 3 'tween deck, buckled the ship's side and

wrecked part of her accommodation. With steam escaping from the boiler and engine room and a loss of power and steering, collision with a damaged vessel immediately ahead was only narrowly avoided. Towed initially by the corvette HMS *Saxifrage*, then by HM tug *Charon*, *Samite* arrived at Algiers early on 6th October, only to sustain further damage in a collision with the London-registered tanker *British Glory*. At Algiers until 20th December, work costing $290,000 included the renewal of eight shell plates, repairs to number 3 hold and to her upper and navigating bridges and the provision of a new anchor and two cargo booms.

10th November 1943: *Sambo* and *Samblade*

Departing Aden that morning for the final sector of her outward maiden voyage from Tocopilla (Chile) to Suez, with a main cargo of 8,850 tons of nitrate, *Sambo* was approaching the southern end of the Red Sea in position 12.28 north by 43.31 east at 15.40, when she was struck on her starboard side by a torpedo from the Japanese submarine *I-27*. Firstly, the vessel's magazine, followed immediately by the nitrate in number 4 hold, violently exploded, shattering the vessel's after part and causing her to sink by the stern within 10 minutes. Of the four lifeboats originally carried, one had been lost in heavy weather in the Pacific, a second was damaged in the explosion and a third capsized

Seen in the Scheldt carrying military vehicles on deck, *Samblade* was subjected to enemy fire in the Gulf of Aden during her maiden voyage in November 1943.*[Photo GVM/Copyright Flor Van Otterdyk]*

during the abandon ship procedures, throwing its occupants into the water and drowning two of them. Ten other crew members were missing but the remaining 35 were rescued by the Norwegian *Helgoy*. Within one hour of *Sambo* being sunk, *Samblade*, sailing between Fremantle and Aden on passage to Suez, carrying military vehicles and 9,000 tons of Chilean nitrate, came under fire from a surfaced submarine three to four miles astern of her position in the Gulf of Aden. Unable to identify the target clearly, no return fire was commenced and the incoming shells ceased immediately a Catalina flying boat and Royal Navy destroyer reached the scene.

18th November 1943: *Sambridge*

Having discharged her main cargo at Madras, the vessel was destined for a US east coast port to reload for the Middle East. On board as she sailed through the Gulf of Aden were 53 crew members, 11 gunners, 200 tons of hides, 165 tons of general cargo and 1,000 tons of sand ballast. When in position 11.25 north by 47.25 east at 18.55, a torpedo from the Japanese submarine *I-27* struck the starboard side of her engine room. One of her boilers exploded; her main engines and two lifeboats were destroyed and fire swept through her accommodation and engine room. One of the two remaining lifeboats was lowered without permission, with only nine aboard, and the rest of the crew, except for three missing men, joined the fourth lifeboat and the rafts. Following a further explosion on her port side, the vessel sank at 19.30, after which *I-27* surfaced and, approaching the lifeboats, demanded that a senior officer board the submarine. In the hope that the request would not be pursued, the Japanese were misled into believing no senior officer had survived. However, on realising their determination to take a prisoner, an injured greaser, the severity of his wounds causing skin to hang off his back, volunteered but was mockingly pushed

back into the lifeboat by the submarine crew. Finally, the Second Officer offered himself and disappeared into the conning tower on his way to a Japanese prison camp. As the submarine moved away, its machine-guns opened fire on the survivors but no injuries resulted. Although one man died from exposure, the others were rescued. *I-27* was also responsible for the sinking of *Sambo* eight days earlier.

26th January 1944: *Samouri*

The ship was sailing to Aden in ballast, on passage from Bombay to the US east coast to reload for India, when, about 95 miles north-east of the island of Socotra at 05.00, a torpedo track was spotted. The vessel's helm was put hard over but it was too late to prevent an explosion on the port side of number 4 hold. The torpedo from *U 188* demolished the ship's number 4 derricks, brought down her main topmast and caused the after deck to become awash. All 39 crew members and 10 gunners took to the four lifeboats before the vessel went down by the stern, the bow remaining upright for a few final minutes before turning slightly round as it slid under at 05.40. The occupants of three lifeboats were rescued next day by the London-registered *Shahzada*, which put them ashore at Aden: the fourth boat became separated and made land at Socotra.

20th April 1944: *Samite*

On her first eastbound sailing from the USA since being damaged some six months previously, the ship was in an 130-ship convoy (UGS 38) in the same general area as in the 1943 attack. In position 37.02 north by 03.41 east at 21.01, an aerial torpedo ripped a 40 by 15 foot hole in the starboard side of number 2 hold, causing a large column of water to swamp the forward part of the vessel and throwing wreckage onto the boat deck abaft the funnel. As a result of the explosion, number 2 hold was flooded to 'tween

Samite made two transAtlantic crossings to the Mediterranean in 1943-44 and on both occasions was severely damaged in air attacks. [Photo GVM/Copyright Flor Van Otterdyk]

deck level, sea entered numbers 1 and 3 and the vessel was so severely down by the head that her propeller boss rose clear of the water. Despite all this, no casualties occurred amongst the crew of 41 and 10 naval gunners and, early next day, the salvage tug *Vagrant* started to tow the vessel the 40 miles to Algiers. There, except for the tangled wreckage of 40-50 cased trucks, she discharged her 3,100 tons of military cargo, which had been loaded in New York and was destined for the Adriatic port of Bari. Under tow once again, on 19th June she was brought into Oran, Algeria where temporary repair work, undertaken by the US Navy in floating dock from 4th to 26th August, enabled her to leave again on 30th September. The vessel sailed to the UK, carrying phosphate in bulk, and subsequently proceeded to New York. Loaded with cargo, *Samite* briefly grounded on sailing for India on 18th January 1945 and the combination of this and the ship's poor condition as a result of her previous damage, created a bottom leak too large to patch. Consequently her cargo was discharged and her sailing from New York postponed until permanent repairs had been completed six weeks later.

6th June 1944: *Sambut*

With 562 troops accommodated in her 'tween decks aft and her holds and decks loaded with vehicles, *Sambut* left London and was due to reach Juno beachhead at Normandy on D+1 Day (7th June). However, when she was east of the Goodwin Sands on D-Day, her convoy (ETM 1) was subjected to bombardment from German 16-inch guns on the French coast. Of the four shells fired, the first two exploded harmlessly in the sea 100 yards from *Sambut*'s port quarter but the third and fourth blew holes in the vessel's port side above the water-line, destroying the two port lifeboats and setting fire to ammunition and cased petrol stowed in vehicles on the forward deck. At 12.15 a vehicle on number 2 hatch exploded with such violence that the ship's bridge was wrecked. Sixty crew members and gunners were instructed to abandon ship in the two undamaged starboard lifeboats, while the troops were ordered to jump into the sea, then utilise the 30 rafts provided for them. The Master, Chief Officer and pilot followed them overboard at 12.40 but two ship's engineers, a seaman and 130 military personnel lost their lives. Although occurring many miles from Normandy, *Sambut* was the first merchant ship loss of the Normandy operation, which involved 21 other 'Sam' ships that summer, 15 carrying vehicles and six transporting stores.

24th July 1944: *Samneva*

After leaving Normandy's Juno beachhead for the Thames in convoy (FTM 47), the vessel was 27 miles south of Selsey Bill at 21.15 when she was struck on her port side by a torpedo from *U 309*. The explosion buckled her decks and sides; blew hatch boards on top of her bridge; disintegrated number 2 lifeboat and flooded holds 2 and 3 to 'tween deck level. The vessel started to settle by the head with a hole 40 feet long fore and aft and 22 feet vertically, extending to her starboard side, and

Sambut was hit by long-range gunfire on 6th June 1944 whilst on passage to Normandy. *[National Maritime Museum, D755]*

severe vibration necessitated that the engines be stopped. A number of the crew of 52 and 18 gunners were injured and non-essential personnel were transferred to a trawler. At 06.20 next day towage was commenced initially by the tug *Owl* and later also by *Amsterdam*, with the result that Cowes Roads were reached at 17.00 and a pump rigged in number 1 hold, by then also leaking. The vessel was beached in Southampton Water but broke in two. While the bow section was subsequently broken up there, the stern part was, in 1947, towed to Swansea Bay by the tug *Twyford* and reached the breakers' yard at Briton Ferry on 14th October, after being involuntarily aground for 11 days in the River Neath.

After being torpedoed, *Samneva* was beached on Netley Sands, where the bow section is being demolished during June 1948. *[D.H. Johnzon/Ships in Focus collection]*

31st July 1944: *Samwake*

Undertaking her first round trip carrying military vehicles from London to Juno beachhead, *Samwake* left Normandy for London in convoy (FTM 53) at 10.00 on 30th July and was later notified by a destroyer of the possibility of enemy attack. This attack duly materialised at 01.30 on 31st July, when an E-boat torpedo ripped into the port side of number 2 hold, not only creating a hole 10 feet long and 10-12 feet deep but also causing an outward bulge in her starboard side. With the ship rapidly listing and holds 1 and 3 also filling with water, the four lifeboats were lowered at 02.50 with all 59 crew and gunners aboard: as the ship was still afloat at 04.30, the Master and six crew members reboarded but before long they were ordered off as *Samwake* began to tip by the head: her stern then reared up vertically, she slowly rolled over to starboard and had totally disappeared by 05.45.

3rd August 1944: *Samlong*

The ship had arrived at Normandy's Gold beachhead with military stores from London on 11th July and had moved six days later to discharge at Sword, where she was splinter damaged by a shell exploding 30 feet away. At 05.35 on 3rd August she was in the convoy anchorage, in preparation for her return to the Thames, when a one-man torpedo blew a 30-foot hole in her starboard side, wrecking and flooding both engine and boiler rooms. The explosion buckled her upper deck and side, forward of the bridge, down as far as 'tween deck level; blew both starboard lifeboats onto the monkey island and killed two engine room crew, the body of one not being discovered for more than three weeks. At 06.50 all, except three senior deck officers and two seamen, transferred in the remaining two lifeboats to HM cruiser *Frobisher*. However, as *Samlong* had remained afloat, the crew re-boarded their vessel to find, to their utter disgust, that, in their absence, their personal belongings had been looted by the crews of the salvage ships *Salveda* and *Salvage Chieftain*. On 5th August a heavy swell was seen to be causing further buckling of the decks, so all crew not required for towing were transferred, mainly to HM landing ship *LST239*, and, the following day, the tug *Allegiance* commenced a tow. The ships passed Dover on 7th August and all went well until just after midnight when, in thick fog, the tug suddenly sheared off and the tow rope, fouling an obstruction, parted, leaving *Samlong* to drift into a partially submerged wreck which, for an hour, became jammed in the gaping hole in her side. Finally freed and able to drop her starboard anchor, she was reunited with *Allegiance*, her anchor was weighed at 18.00 on 8th August and the tug and her tow safely negotiated the Thames as far as Greenhithe the following day. On 11th November *Samlong* was towed to the River Blackwater in Essex, the intention being that she would be sent to the Tyne for permanent repairs but, in 1947, she was condemned as a hulk and consequently saw no further service.

5th August 1944: *Samsylarna*

On passage from New York to Bombay, Colombo and Calcutta, initially in convoy (UGS 48), *Samsylarna* was hit by an aerial torpedo off the North African coast. With her engine room and number 5 hold completely flooded and number 4 hold partially so, she went aground at Benghazi (Libya) but, after pumping operations and the transfer of 600 tons of cargo to lighters and to the coaster *Lanrick*, she was refloated with a gaping hole in number 5. Devoid of a stern frame, propeller and rudder, she was taken in tow but, in heavy weather, developed a leak in number 3 hold. After calling into Tobruk (Libya) for temporary repairs, she reached Alexandria on 24th September. The extent of the damage made her unfit for further service and beyond local repair, so the British intention was that she should be returned to the Americans, who, in early 1945, considered her for employment as a floating storage hulk, which would have required the use of her winches and booms. No repairs were carried out and she was returned to the US Maritime Commission in 1949 as a hulk. Surprisingly, in view of her condition, two years later she was towed to Genoa under the new name *Tito Campanella*, for service under the Italian flag.

Despite serious damage in 1944 and being written off five years later, *Samsylarna* was rebuilt and is shown here in July 1969 as the Polish *Huto Sosnowiec*. Amongst a number of modifications are the bridge front and funnel. *[John G. Callis/Ships in Focus collection]*

18th August 1944: *Samdel*

Whilst berthed at C Shed, South West India Dock, London after completing seven round voyages to the Normandy beachheads, the ship was hit on the port quarter by a German V1 flying bomb at 07.17, causing number 5 hold to become flooded, the vessel's stern to settle on the bottom and seven gunners to sustain injuries. Because of the extensive damage, it was not until 31st December that she was in a fit state to start her next voyage – to Milford Haven and New York.

29th September 1944: *Samsuva*

After discharging her military cargo, the vessel was released to load timber for the UK and left Archangel on 26th September. About 100 miles off North Cape at 16.15 on 29th September she was showered with debris from an explosion aboard the US-flag *Edward H. Crockett* immediately ahead in the convoy (RA 60) and *Samsuva*'s rudder then jammed while being put hard over to avoid a collision. Nineteen minutes later, in position 72.58 north by 23.59 east, a torpedo from *U 310* blasted a 15-foot circular hole in the starboard side of her engine room, opened an 18-inch split in her port side from the main deck to below water level, demolished number 3 lifeboat and caused her funnel to belch steam, smoke, soot and cordite fumes with a tremendous roar. Three crew died in the explosion but the remaining 37 and 20 gunners, including two with injuries, boarded rafts and the three surviving lifeboats and were picked up by the convoy rescue vessel *Rathlin*. Aided by shells from a Royal Navy destroyer, thought to have been *Scorpion*, *Samsuva* was last observed to be burning furiously, with her bows high in the air. The eight other 'Sam' ships in the convoy – *Samannan*, *Samcalia*, *Samconstant*, *Samgara*, *Samidway*, *Samloyal*, *Samlyth* and *Samtredy* – all reached the UK unscathed and their British sister ships – *Adolph S. Ochs* and *Samaritan* – each survived three other North Russian convoys.

5th December 1944: *Samtana* and *Samnethy*

In an unsuccessful attempt to prevent a collision in the North Sea with *Samnethy*, *Samtana* went aground and was then struck on her starboard side, level with her foremast, by *Samnethy*, which herself then grounded. *Samtana* refloated on the flood tide after two hours and reached the Tyne on 10th December but initial attempts to refloat *Samnethy*, which was carrying 8,750 tons of iron ore, failed despite the attendance of three tugs; her starboard bower anchor being laid out and 150 tons of fuel oil being jettisoned. On 10th December, pounding heavily, she shifted in a gale and, with the possibility that their ship might break up, the crew were landed at Great Yarmouth. However, she did finally refloat that day and, with buckling beside number 2 hold, was towed by the tugs *Prizeman* and *Irishman* to reach Middlesbrough on 16th December where she remained until sailing for the Eastern Mediterranean on 20th November 1945.

Samsip is seen leaving New York for India on 12th December 1943 at the start of a career which was ended by a mine less than a year later. *[D.H. Johnzon collection]*

7th December 1944: *Samsip*

Returning to the Thames from Antwerp in convoy (ATM 6) but sailing outside the swept channel in the vicinity of Ostend, the vessel struck a mine at 21.43. With her back broken abaft the bridge, she was engulfed in flames from midships to stern, the explosion taking the lives of an engineer, fireman and greaser in the engine room and of two officers who were found dead in their cabins. HM *MTB 729* went alongside her port bow to rescue dazed and badly injured men and *MTB 753* found others on rafts drifting astern of the ship: one man hit his head on the ship's side and disappeared in the water during the rescue. The destroyer HMS *Fernie* and HM trawler *Alfredian* were on the scene, the former reporting that, by 02.20 next day, the vessel had sunk down to her gunwhales, with ammunition starting to explode as the fire spread to the fore end of the ship. She was a total loss with her central section resting on the bottom and her bow and stern initially remaining afloat at a steep angle.

11th December 1944: *Samtucky*

Two days after leaving New York carrying 6,000 tons of general cargo and 611 tons of ammunition, the vessel experienced failure in both feed pumps but initially remained in convoy (HX 325) for protection, while one pump was restored. On 13th December she put into Halifax, where she was declared unseaworthy until repairs enabled her to leave on 21st December. After joining a Liverpool-bound convoy (HX 327), at 16.10 that day a 40 by 20-foot hole was ripped in her starboard side abreast number 4 hatch by a torpedo from *U 806*. Sea water started washing over the after deck as holds 4 and 5 flooded and, with the water level rising, a boiler explosion was feared. The vessel was steered towards the shoals, with the port anchor being let go to keep her head to sea until help arrived in the form of a corvette, whose towing line immediately parted, and the tug *Bersimis*, which succeeded in damaging the ship's starboard lifeboats. Two additional tugs, *Foundation Security* and *Banscot*, arrived on the scene but the parting of the forward tow rope resulted in *Samtucky* going securely aground at 04.30 on 22nd December. Pumping out was commenced and, using a floating crane to discharge cargo from the after deck, the ship refloated two days later and returned to Halifax, where she remained until her 10th August 1945 departure for Philadelphia to load for French Gironde ports.

Her damage repaired, *Samtucky* was photographed in the Scheldt post-war, after the removal of her guns but not their bandstands. *[Photo GVM/Copyright Flor Van Otterdyk]*

18th January 1945: *Samvern*

At the start of the return leg of her fourth round voyage between London and Antwerp, the ship was in convoy (ATM 41) when a mine strike five miles north west of Zeebrugge broke her in two. Thirty-nine survivors were rescued by HM landing ship *LST239* and a further six by the destroyer *Fernie*. Nine members of the crew, including the Bosun, lost their lives, as did five Army tank drivers and the London and Belgian pilots.

27th February 1945: *Sampa*

When north of Ostend in convoy (ATM 77) from Antwerp to London at 17.12, a mine explosion blew the Master from the bridge into the sea and killed nine crew members, four gunners, the Dutch pilot and an RAF serviceman travelling as a passenger. Survivors were picked up by HM destroyer *Middleton*. The US landing ship *LST532* stood by and the tug *Empire Betsy* and salvage vessel *Lincoln Salvor* were despatched to save the ship but to no avail.

19th March 1945: *Samselbu*

This vessel became another 'Sam' ship mine victim in the same area north of Ostend. She sailed from Antwerp for London at 07.10 and, whilst in convoy (ATM 97) at 18.22, the explosion detached her stern, which floated away and sank, leaving the bridge and fore part undamaged but doomed. One of her crew members was killed and seven were injured. At 19.10 the ship was abandoned and most of the survivors were rescued by HM landing craft *LCT366*. The hulk was last reported as having its after end touching bottom at an angle of 35°.

9th-10th April 1945: *Samida*

In convoy (TBC 123) nine miles north east of Dungeness, on passage in ballast from Antwerp to Swansea and New York, *Samida* was torpedoed by a midget submarine at 22.00 on 9th April. Struck on her starboard side at number 5 hold,

With her back broken, *Sampa* is doomed as a result of a mine explosion whilst on passage from Antwerp to London in ballast. *[D.H. Johnzon collection]*

the vessel rapidly settled by the stern with her starboard lifeboats smashed, engine room flooded and engines and rudder out of action. Her Master was one of seven men to sustain minor injuries but there were no fatalities and all 57 men were landed by naval trawler at Dover. When she went down at 02.00 on 10th April, *Samida* became the fifth 'Sam' ship to be sunk whilst outward bound from Antwerp.

14th April 1945: *Samspelga* and *Samjack*

After arriving in the same convoy (MKS 93) from Casablanca and Gibraltar respectively, *Samspelga* sustained extensive bow damage in a collision with *Samjack* off the Kent coast. The *Samjack's* starboard side was affected over a 10 by 6 foot area abreast number 4 hold but both ships were able to complete their voyages to Hull. Repairs to *Samjack* lasted six weeks and to *Samspelga's* stem three months.

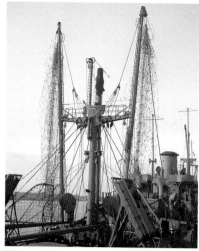 

Detail of *Samwater's* anti-torpedo nets (left) and raft (right). She survived the war only to be lost by fire in 1947. *[Photo GVM/Copyright Flor Van Otterdyk]*

30th April 1945: *Samclyde*

At the end of a voyage from St. John (New Brunswick), *Samclyde* was approaching Salonica Bay (Greece) at 13.48 when a mine exploded abreast number 1 hold on the port side. Her engines were stopped and, by 14.00, the vessel was settling so rapidly by the head that the crew were ordered into the lifeboats and two were cast off. Although drifting well into the minefield, the vessel had ceased to settle by 14.30, so the crew re-boarded and, within half an hour, *Samclyde* had been guided to safety by a fishing boat and, ready to beach if necessary, anchored in Salonica Bay at 19.08. The ship left on 27th May for Alexandria, where she stayed until sailing for South Shields on 3rd August. In need of extensive repairs, she remained in the Tyne until her sailing date of 7th May 1946, her destination being Hampton Roads (Virginia) for lay-up.

20th May 1945: *Samlistar*

Bound from Montreal to the UK, *Samlistar* grounded on rocks in an exposed position five miles off Sydney (Nova Scotia). The jettisioning of 1,250 tons of grain cargo enabled her to refloat after five days with the aid of the salvage tug *Foundation Franklin*. After calling at Sydney, she left with tug escort for Quebec to discharge all remaining cargo and for 32 bottom and shell plates to be renewed in drydock, completion of which enabled her to leave on 10th August.

29th January 1947: *Samwater*

Nearing the end of her voyage carrying wool from Sydney to Liverpool and Antwerp, *Samwater* was in position 42.41 north by 10.13 west 35 miles west of Cape Finisterre (Spain). Fire broke out in the engine room while the crew were carrying out repairs, and spread so rapidly that, with it being impossible to reduce the vessel's speed, all aboard were ordered to abandon ship. In the heavy seas, two lifeboats capsized, drowning 16 crew and two passengers but the Master, 22 crew and three passengers were picked up by the Swedish *P.L. Pahlsson* and landed at Lisbon. The following day the ship was still afloat with her four forward holds burning furiously and she was six feet down by the stern. Despite *Witte Zee* being joined by another Dutch tug, *Thames*, on 2nd February, the storm drove *Samwater* ashore near Carballo (Spain), with only her forepart visible and within two days even this had disappeared in deep water.

Samtampa during her wartime service. Her career ended tragically in an April 1947 gale. *[D. H. Johnzon/Roy Fenton collection]*

Three views of the wreck of *Samtampa*, lost with all hands in the Bristol Channel. Eight Mumbles lifeboatmen also perished in the disaster. *[South Wales Echo and Mail/National Waterfront Museum]*

23rd April 1947: *Samtampa*

On a voyage from Middlesbrough to Newport in ballast, the ship had both anchors down in position 51.19 north by 03.45 west owing to heavy seas in a gale-swept Bristol Channel. The carrying away of the starboard anchor, followed 20 minutes later by the parting of the port one, resulted in the vessel drifting ashore at Porthcawl and breaking into three sections. All 39 aboard were lost, as was the eight-man crew of the Mumbles lifeboat, which, in making a rescue attempt, had been overwhelmed and was found capsized near the wreck of *Samtampa*.

25th August 1947: *Sampep*

A major fire which engulfed the dock at Port Alberni (Western Canada) spread to *Sampep*; she was towed away with her deck cargo of lumber and her bridge alight and the blaze also affecting holds 4 and 5. Still burning, on 29th August the vessel moved to Victoria under her own power but with the tug *Salvage Chieftain* in attendance. By this time, her midship accommodation was damaged; plating had become buckled; her two starboard lifeboats had been rendered useless and there was contamination in the wheat and lumber in her three after holds. Discharge of her cargo

169

and repairs meant that it was 10th December before she was again ready to leave Victoria.

31st January 1948: *Samkey*
After the vessel left London on 24th January with 1,500 tons of stone and sand ballast, she was expected to reach Cuba about 11th February. She transmitted a report of a Force 6 south-westerly gale from position 41.48 north 24.00 west, north-east of the Azores, at 13.45 on 31st January and nothing was ever heard of her again. Frequent radio enquiries from *Port Chalmers* between 4th and 18th February went unanswered and, on the 20th, an air search was called for from the Azores. No further news being forthcoming, she was posted as missing: the cause of her loss, with all hands, was put down to the sudden shifting of her ballast.

To be concluded.

A post-war photograph of *Sampep* which, in 1947 (right), became engulfed by a dock fire at Port Alberni, Western Canada. *[Roy Fenton collection]*

Whilst crossing a gale-swept Atlantic in ballast during early 1948, *Samkey,* seen here at 15 South Wharf, Melbourne, was lost without trace. *[Russell Priest collection]*

SOURCES AND ACKNOWLEDGEMENTS

We thank all who gave permission for their photographs to be used, and for help in finding photographs we are particularly grateful to Tony Smith, Jim McFaul and David Whiteside of the World Ship Photo Library; to Ian Farquhar, F.W. Hawks, Peter Newall, William Schell, George Scott; and to David Hodge and Bob Todd of the National Maritime Museum, and other museums and institutions listed.

Research sources have included the *Registers* of William Schell and Tony Starke, *Lloyd's Register*, *Lloyd's Confidential Index*, *Lloyd's War Losses*, *Mercantile Navy Lists*, *Marine News* and *Shipbuilding and Shipping Record*. Use of the facilities of the World Ship Society, the Guildhall Library, the National Archives and Lloyd's Register of Shipping and the help of Dr Malcolm Cooper are gratefully acknowledged. Particular thanks also to Heather Fenton for editorial and indexing work, and to Marion Clarkson for her accountancy services.

Clunies
The author wishes to acknowledge the assistance of Mrs Margaret Johnston in the preparation of this article, and to the publishers of 'Marine Propulsion' for permission to quote from an article by Ian Muir in their February 1996 issue.

Merchant aircraft carrier-grain ships
Mr J. Lenaghan read the paper 'Merchant Aircraft Carrier Ships ('MAC' Ships)' to the Institution of Naval Architects in 1946. As Personal Assistant (Technical) to the Controller of Merchant Shipbuilding and Repair at the Admiralty, Lenaghan was deeply involved in the design of the ships, and many of the others involved contributed to the discussion. The article is based on the paper and subsequent discussion.

EVERY PICTURE...AT YARMOUTH

Not only is this a delightful pictorial scene, it also has many features of interest. The photographer is recorded on the back as C.R. Temple of Norwich, the location is Yarmouth, and the writer admits to some surprise that the port could take a 4,119 gt steamer like *Pearlmoor*. Oblique views like this have the advantage of showing the remarkable cross-sectional shape of a Doxford Turret.

At least four varieties of other craft are visible, including to far left and far right, Thames spritsail barges. Moving left we have a smaller local sailing craft, perhaps a wherry, and next left a very elderly (judging by the height of her funnel) steamer. Almost obscured is a topsail schooner with a white hull, probably from Scandinavia.

Pearlmoor's managers, Walter Runciman and Company of Newcastle-upon-Tyne, were one of the biggest operators of Turrets, ordering 11, including the last one that Doxford built, the *Orangemoor* of 1911 (yard number 423). They had two named *Pearlmoor;* the first, Doxford's yard number 257, was built in 1897 and lost in 1904. This makes it more likely that the photo depicts her replacement, yard number 349, completed in 1905 and in the Runciman fleet until 1919 when she became *Pearlmead* of Western Counties Shipping Co. Ltd. The second photograph, taken by Raul Maya of her arriving at Montevideo in 1938 as *Uru*, helps to confirm this identification, as features such as the offset steam pipe behind the funnel and the angled supports for the bridge are visible in both photographs.

Pearlmead's stay with the rather unfortunate Western Counties company of Cardiff was short, and in 1922 she was sold to F.V. Eberhardt of London, whose name might indicate a distant connection with a once well-known coaster owner. Eberhardt quickly sold her on to Karck and Knott who also disposed of her within the year to Emder Reederei A.G. of Germany who changed her name from *Pearlmead* to *Anneliese*. A final renaming to *Uru* marked her sale to Lloyd Brasiliero in 1925. She stayed with the Brazilian owner until 1957 when she was broken up at Rio, putting her amongst the last half dozen of Turrets to survive.

A detailed look at *Pearlmoor* reveals some further features, including what is presumably a discharge pipe on the port side aft, carried well above the harbour deck. Further forward on this deck are a couple of small boats, possibly belonging to the repairers who are working on her hull right aft, taking advantage of her being very light. Indeed, her propellor boss can just be seen.

THE SHORT-LIVED CLUNIES STEAMSHIP COMPANY

Archie Munro

In 'Record' 39 I wrote the obituary to a very good friend and dedicated archivist for much of Clydeside's industrial past, the late Dr William Lind. Just before his death, Bill and I had been reminiscing on the brief period in the late 1940s when the Clunies Company had not only come into existence but also passed into history on the Greenock waterfront, at a time when both of us had begun our working lives in that same area.

Origins

To understand the origins of the Clunies Company, it is necessary to first refer to two names believed to have been involved in its creation and who began their separate working lives in the second half of the 19th century. James Clunies, whose great grandfather came from Shetland, was born in Glasgow in 1857 and became in turn a railway clerk, an iron merchant and an accountant. He married in Glasgow in 1878 from which resulted a family of 14 but not all survived beyond an early age. By 1915 James Clunies was a man of some means and bought a large, recently-built house in Gourock, prominently situated on the Ashton Hill with a commanding view over the lochs and upper Firth of Clyde. Clunies' wife died there in 1938 followed by James Clunies himself three years later at the age of 84, without apparently ever having had any direct connections with shipping throughout his life.

The other principal in this story was John Johnston, born in the Shawlands district of Glasgow in 1888, who in 1914 was employed as a chartering clerk and shipbroker with the firm of Mann, Macneal and Company. In 1915 he married Margaret Thomson Clunies, a daughter of James Clunies, and went to live with his in-laws in Gourock where they were to bring up three sons. In 1915 John Johnston also set up in business with one Carl Olsen (previously employed with a firm of coal exporters), as Olsen, Johnston and Company, shipbrokers and general agents, in Wellington Street, Glasgow. Late in 1917 these two men took over the ailing Larne Shipbuilding Company in Northern Ireland, reformed it as a limited company and laid out a larger slipway complex able to accommodate ships up to 1,000 tons, but only three coasters appear to have been built there before the yard closed down in March 1921; the last ship having been completed in Glasgow.

Meanwhile the Olsen, Johnston company continued its Glasgow business which in 1922 became a limited

Dr John Johnston, 1888-1957, principal of Olsen, Johnston and the Clunies Shipping Company. *[Mrs Margaret Johnstone]*

company and five years later moved to more prestigious offices at 3 Royal Exchange Square, while in 1931 Olsen left to join a firm of coal and coke exporters, although his name remained with the company until its ultimate demise nearly half a century later. Each of the Johnston sons was to become part of the Olsen, Johnston company, except during and after the Second World War when they served in the Army, while John Johnston continued as principal of the firm until he died in 1957, being then succeeded by his eldest son, John Clunies Johnston. As shipping agents in Glasgow, the company survived until the rundown of the port and its facilities in the late 1970s.

At the end of the Second World War and with the gradual return to peacetime trading in 1945, Olsen, Johnston and its principal were able to look back on thirty years' experience in the shipping industry acting as owners' agents and were thoroughly versed in ships' business, including chartering in the world of tramp shipping. John Johnston was then aged 57, his wife Margaret T. Clunies was 54, and their eldest son, John C. Johnston, 29.

Surplus ships

In 1946 it became apparent that certain types of ships would be surplus to requirements and available for purchase with the prospect of profitable trading while the worldwide demand for ships and cargoes remained high. Large numbers of US, Canadian and British government tonnage (e.g. Liberties, Empires, Oceans, Forts and Parks) were initially offered to ship owners who had lost ships during the war and required to resume the peacetime pattern of their trades as quickly as possible. However, some of these surplus ships remained unsold by the summer of 1947; notably two of the grain-carrying *Empire Mac* class of carriers which were less attractive to prospective owners by reason of their retained and cumbersome flight deck structures, although this did not prevent them continuing to carry Canadian grain cargoes into Liverpool. Olsen, Johnston became shipowners on 1st October 1947 by purchasing *Empire MacCallum*, then in Liverpool, and appointed Captain J.G. Stephenson as Master to take over the ship from the Hain Steamship Co. Ltd. who had managed her since completion in 1943. She sailed next day for Montreal, returned with another grain cargo four weeks later and, during eight days in port discharging, was re-named *Doris Clunies* and sailed as such for Halifax on 12th December. It is believed the name 'Doris' was taken from the wife of Captain Boxberg who was acting as Marine

Superintendent for the owners, and who later became a director of the company.

The purchase of *Empire MacCallum* was arranged concurrently with two other ships bought through the Ministry of Transport from the Admiralty, who in 1946 decided to dispose of all seven of the C-type Empire ships ordered from Sunderland shipyards in 1944 and fitted out to serve as mobile maintenance bases for the fleet both at home and abroad, of which only two were commissioned before the war in the Far East ended and rendered them virtually surplus to requirement. This caught the attention of the Swedish Captain G.W.L. Boxberg, who then invited John Johnston to join him in a combined bid for the purchase, conversion and management of an unspecified number of these ships. In effect Johnston and his company would provide the necessary backing, financial and otherwise for the entire project while Boxberg prepared the technical specification for the conversion of the ships into cargo ships and thereafter contributed to their management.

HMS *Mullion Cove* was the first of the Empire type to complete and was despatched to Trincomalee to serve with the East Indies Fleet, but left there for home on 2nd February 1946, de-stored in Glasgow during the first week of April and was then laid up in the Holy Loch and clearly visible from the Johnston residence in Gourock. The other completed Empire C-type was HMS *Cuillin Sound* which served as a repair ship at Harwich until placed in reserve and laid up in Barry Docks also during April 1946. At the beginning of 1947 Olsen, Johnston began negotiations for the purchase of both ships which ultimately proved successful.

On 25th August 1947 *Mullion Cove* was moved from the Holy Loch into the James Watt Dock in Greenock to remove ballast and Admiralty equipment and to begin conversion to general cargo status suitable for the bulk cargoes of the tramping trades. In four months this ship had 14 movements to different berths including that on 6th November to the riverside Deep Water Berth and by which date her name had been changed to *Margaret Clunies*. On 28th December she moved to Glasgow for ten days of dry docking before returning to Greenock for a further ten weeks in the James Watt Dock. On 19th March

Empire MacCallum. [National Maritime Museum, P23361]

Dories Clunies was photographed after acquisition but before conversion at an icy Montreal on one of her many visits between May 1948 and July 1949.
[Mrs Margaret Johnstone]

The maintenance ship *Mullion Cove* on 19th July 1945 with a partial cargo of landing craft. *[Frank and Sons/Imperial War Museum]*

Margaret Clunies at Venice on 10th May 1949 having brought a coal cargo from Amsterdam. *[Mrs Margaret Johnstone]*

1948 *Margaret Clunies* finally undocked on completion of a seven-month conversion and after two days of trials and adjustments sailed from the Tail of the Bank for Narvik to load her first cargo, iron ore for Immingham.

The other Empire C-type ship, completed as HMS *Cuillin Sound*, was steamed up from Barry already renamed *James Clunies* and berthed in the James Watt Dock on 16th December 1947, to begin a seven-month conversion along with her sister ship from fleet maintenance ship to general tramp which involved 17 dock movements before undocking on 1st July 1948 and, after completing a day of trials, sailed next day on her maiden voyage in ballast to Wabana in Newfoundland to load ore for Middlesborough. By the year end she had lifted five cargoes but had put into the Tyne for 19 days of repairs in August, and seven days at the Tail of the Bank for repairs and storing in September and, having brought a Cuban sugar cargo to Greenock in November, spent 18 days in that port completing minor voyage repairs.

Nevertheless, by the end of 1948 the company could claim some success in the tramping business. *Doris Clunies* had completed nine Canadian grain cargoes into Liverpool, *Margaret Clunies* five cargoes in nine months including grain from Montreal to Hull and a similar cargo from Rosario to Glasgow. *James Clunies* in five months completed four cargoes including two with phosphates, one from Safi to Hamburg and another from Sfax to Venice.

While the two Empire C-type ships were completing conversion in the first half of 1948, ownership of all three ships was formalised by setting up separate companies to own and manage them from the same office as that of Olsen, Johnston in Glasgow. The *James* and *Margaret Clunies* were registered in the ownership of the Margareta Steamship Co. Ltd., while the Doris Steamship Co. Ltd. became owners of the *Doris Clunies* and the Clunies Steamship Company (unlimited) became managers of all three ships. Only *Doris Clunies* had her port of

Maintenance ship HMS *Cuillin Sound* laid up in Barry on 1st September 1949. *[Hansen Collection 1672/1760, Amgueddfa Cymru – National Museum Wales]*

registry changed to Greenock, the remaining ships of the growing fleet remained with London registry.

The *Marianne Clunies*

It was at this time that negotiations began for a fourth ship to join the Clunies fleet, but surplus from the First World War rather than the Second. After 90 years it is now largely forgotten that in the period 1917-21 the United States set up the 'Fabricated Ship Program' to construct an emergency merchant fleet in eight sizes mainly in the 7,500 to 9,600 deadweight range of which almost 900 were built in shipyards countrywide, including the rather ugly sheerless 'Hog Island' type which emerged from an incredible new yard specially laid out on a green field site across the Delaware River from the Philadelphia Navy Yard. This became then the largest shipyard in the world with a frontage of two miles and slips for 50 ships.

Marianne Clunies in the Great Harbour, Greenock around March 1949 with a modernised bridge front but before fitting a new funnel. *[Mrs Margaret Johnstone]*

The common denominator of these ships was their three-island, counter-stern design with five holds and hatches. Machinery included triple- or quadruple-expansion and geared turbines, all supplied by steam from three oil-fired boilers. They became a familiar enough sight between the wars but having been built in excess of requirements many were laid up on completion and had deteriorated by the outbreak of war in September 1939. Nevertheless, by 1940 the British government was desperate for ships to keep pace with losses and negotiated the purchase of one hundred, which were taken over in the United States during that year and the next. Only a third were immediately serviceable, the remainder needed much in the way of repairs which, due to the dollar shortage, had to be carried out in the UK and added to the pressure on ship repair yards. Some were torpedoed and sunk while en route to the UK.

During the war these old ships served worldwide including on Russian convoys. Whilst managed by British liner and tramp companies, ownership was retained by the Ministry of War Transport throughout. They suffered grievous losses: 53 to enemy action and with 20 stranded, sunk as block ships at Normandy or scuttled post-war with redundant ammunition. A mere 27 survived of which one was returned to the US, eight sold to Allied owners, six to Hong Kong and five to London Greek companies which left eight to be disposed amongst British owners. One of those was immediately broken up and by mid-1948 only *Empire Opossum* remained unsold and possibly viewed as the ship that had been forgotten, yet she was soon to have another lease of life.

Completed at Portland, Oregon in 1918 with the auspicious name of *Western Ocean*, the 30-year old *Empire Opossum* had been managed by G. Heyn and Sons Ltd. of Belfast from 1941 until the end of 1944 when, whilst discharging a grain cargo from Rosario in Glasgow, she was taken up for store ship duties under Admiralty control, and by the third week of December was berthed in the vast Clyde Anchorage. In April 1945 she moved to the Gareloch and later that year to an anchorage off Coulport in Loch Long, being described as an 'Ammo Store Hulk', and remained there until 4th December 1946 when towed to Corpach, close to Fort William on Loch Linnhe, and remained there in isolation for the next two years, but was then towed back to the Clyde and berthed in Greenock's James Watt Dock on 17th December 1948, having just been acquired by Olsen, Johnston. The name *Marianne Clunies* was painted up in March 1949.

Ownership of *Marianne Clunies* was with the James Steamship Co. Ltd. while Clunies continued as managers of all four ships. By the summer of 1949, however, the offices of the managers and all the owning companies were transferred from Glasgow to 193 Dalrymple Street in Greenock, presumably to separate the ship owning

Marianne Clunies on trials, 3rd September 1949: note the new funnel. *[Mrs Margaret Johnstone]*

side of the business from that of the shipping agency, although Olsen, Johnston continued to act as agents for all four ships whenever in Greenock or Glasgow. However, there was another reason for the move to Greenock. During the 1948 conversions of the *Margaret Clunies* and *James Clunies*, much of the work was carried out by the Greenock firm of Caldwell Brothers (Marine) Ltd., who had started up in the ship repair business during the war to serve the mass of shipping then at the Clyde anchorages. They had a machine shop in Roslin Street which was but a few steps from the office of the new ship owners in Dalrymple Street. Caldwell Brothers (Marine) Ltd. were now to become heavily involved in the re-engining of *Marianne Clunies*.

Trading patterns

At this point it is convenient to see how the three Clunies-owned ships were trading. During the first seven months of 1949 *Doris Clunies* continued with her grain voyages to Liverpool, loading in Montreal between May and November and in Halifax during the winter. Throughout these voyages the flight deck and supporting structure was gradually being reduced by embarking on each trip a number of oxy-acetylene burners complete with a suitable supply of gas cylinders. Some of the flight deck sections may have gone overboard but most were saved and landed as valuable scrap in Liverpool when discharging grain. On her 16th voyage, *Doris Clunies* docked in Greenock on 24th July 1949 to remain in the James Watt Dock as a temporary grain store for four months.

The voyages of *Margaret Clunies* in 1949 began on Hogmanay when she sailed from Glasgow to Baltimore and homeward with grain to Liverpool, then Halifax with grain to Avonmouth, phosphates from Casablanca to Rotterdam, then Venice and Trieste with general to Yokohama, returning from British Columbian ports via Panama to Hull, then Finland to Immingham and Hull to Leghorn, which was left on 29th December bound for Casablanca.

The *James Clunies* spent the first two weeks of 1949 discharging phosphates in Venice, then carried a similar cargo from Sfax to Nordenham at the entrance to the River Weser in north west Germany. Her next cargo was coal from Amsterdam to Buenos Aires and proved to be the last that she delivered. The ship was then ordered down the Argentine coast to load grain at the small port of Necochea, where she spent four days but whether any cargo was loaded there is unknown. She then proceeded further down the coast to load in Bahia Blanca and remained there for 12 days completing a full cargo of grain for Italy.

James Clunies departed Bahia Blanca on the morning of 20th April 1949 bound initially for Montevideo where fuel oil bunkers were to be shipped as these were not available at the port of loading. This was to be a relatively straightforward mainly coastal passage of 470 miles occupying 50 hours at 9.5 knots. Maximum draft of the ship was 27 feet 2 inches. When about halfway along the route by next morning, the Chief Officer obtained a running fix position at 07.00 which placed the ship 10.75 miles south south east of Quequen Lighthouse at Necochea. Visibility then must have been more than 11 miles to have allowed the fix and the course then being steered to pass a distance of eight miles off the next headland, Punta Mogotes, appears to have been a safe and reasonable one.

However, the Admiralty Sailing Directions warned of a dangerous rock and sand spit, with a depth of only 18 feet over it, extending two miles to seaward of Punta Mogotes, with another bank of similar depth restriction positioned 2.5 miles south east of that same point and so by passing only eight miles off Mogotes meant 5.5 miles off that bank. Had the visibility remained clear the ship may well have passed Punta Mogotes clear of danger, but by noon the weather was reported as east north east force 5, sea moderate, visibility variable but poor during intermittent rain. Even allowing for a little set towards the coast in the strengthening offshore wind, the ship might still have passed clear, but at 11.00 course was altered 13 degrees to port, presumably to close the land in an attempt to ascertain the position, but this course allowed barely half a mile clearance from the outer edge of the bank while the wind would clearly set the vessel much closer still. In the event no land was seen until Punta Mogotes Lighthouse and a line of breakers was suddenly sighted on the port hand. The ship stranded virtually at the same instant before any avoiding action could be taken. All 44 crew were safely taken off, the ship soon broke in two and was declared a constructive total loss. The wreck disappeared in the gales of 1950.

The Macleod turbine

The loss of this fine four-year-old ship must have been a severe blow to the relatively new company struggling to establish itself in a very competitive world market. Four months earlier they had seen their fourth ship into the James Watt Dock where work began on reconditioning to make good the past four years of neglect and, having been towed to and from Corpach, *Empire Opossum* was obviously in need of much attention in the engine room. The ship was fitted with the original double-reduction geared turbine manufactured by the General Electric

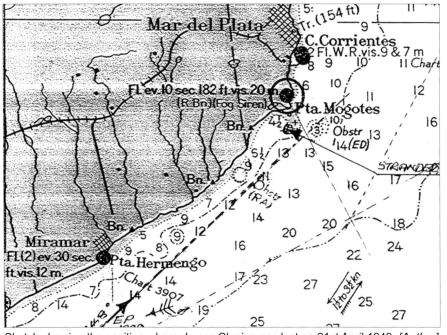

Sketch showing the position where *James Clunies* was lost on 21st April 1949. [*Author*]

Empire Opossum on 26th October 1942. *[Ian J. Farquhar collection]*

Company in Schenectady, New York State. At this point an inventive engineer joins the story.

Just before the First World War, a Glasgow engineer, James MacLeod, tried to interest the North British Locomotive Company (NBL) at Springburn, Glasgow in applying geared steam turbines to railway locomotives, but the war intervened and it was 1921 before MacLeod and the NBL took out joint patents on the project. Such a loco was indeed exhibited at Wembley in 1924 but got no further. In 1936 the MacLeod Steam Turbine Company was registered in Glasgow and by 1939 it was announced that MacLeod had actually designed, built and tested a revolutionary marine turbine offering distinct savings in fuel and weight, but once again a war interfered with further progress at that time.

Towards the end of the Second World War, however, questions were being asked in Parliament as to why the MacLeod steam turbine had not been tried out at sea, following the successful bench trials in 1939. On 16th May 1945 the Member for Pollok actually asked 'Why has it not been fitted in the *Empire Opossum*, at present lying in the Gareloch with broken-down main engines, particularly when the managers of this ship (i.e. the Admiralty) have indicated their willingness to install this unit and a prominent Glasgow engineering firm is willing to undertake installation?'

It seems reasonable to suppose, therefore, that the decision to install and test at sea the MacLeod steam turbine was a joint venture by the Admiralty and the prospective new owners of the *Empire Opossum* faced with broken down machinery. It has also been suggested that James MacLeod was introduced to the owners by Captain Boxberg. At any rate, following arrival on 17th December 1948, this ship spent 62 days in the James Watt Dock, making five shifts in the process which presumably involved the 150-ton crane removing the original turbine. She then moved to the Victoria Harbour for 34 days with one shift which may have involved that 75-ton crane lifting aboard the MacLeod turbine, which had actually been manufactured

by a Birmingham engineering firm, Bellis and Morcom Ltd., in 1939. Thereafter she moved to a quieter berth at the Great Harbour and remained there for four months. On 14th July she moved into the Garvel Drydock for fifteen days cleaning, painting and possibly propeller change, then returned to the Great Harbour for five weeks of final fittings and adjustments and where renaming to *Marianne Clunies* also took place. The name change was registered on 30th August, but had actually been sanctioned by the Board of Trade as far back as March.

The total conversion, which included the fitting of a modernised bridge structure and funnel, occupied a period of almost nine months. Most, if not all, of the engineering work appears to have been carried out by Caldwell Brothers (Marine) Ltd. At 06.45 on 3rd September 1949 the *Marianne Clunies* left her berth for a preliminary trial on the Firth; some observers noting that they only saw her at slow speed but she returned to her berth alongside that same evening for a further four days of adjustments. Then at 13.00 on the 7th she again proceeded on trial and that evening returned to the anchorage at the Tail of the Bank where the main party of officials and observers landed while another squad of engineers boarded to work through the night. Both MacLeod and Johnston boarded the ship first thing next morning, and by the morning of the 10th it was decided the ship required to return to the Great Harbour and she berthed there that afternoon.

The *Marianne Clunies* proceeded on further trials in the early hours of the 12th, spent all of the next two days at the anchorage with much to-ing and fro-ing with engineers from Caldwell Brothers, then returned to the Great Harbour in the evening of the 14th and this time the ship remained on the berth for 17 days. On 1st October she emerged again and proceeded on an extended trial but returned to the anchorage on the morning of the 5th. During the next seven days at anchor, there were intense movements involving Caldwell Brothers' engineers, surveyors, the Captain, Chief Engineer, Johnston and MacLeod, including the shipment of welding plant, gas cylinders and all manner of tools and equipment. Finally at 05.00 on 12th October the *Marianne* returned to a berth in the James Watt Dock and was presumably accepted for service with the MacLeod turbine within the next few days. She made one shift in the dock then, at 11.00 on Wednesday 19th October, she cleared out and sailed for Casablanca, ostensibly to load a cargo of phosphates.

Two days out from the Clyde, *Marianne Clunies* reported to Lands End Radio that she had 'pump trouble' and six days later reported 'turbine trouble' to Portishead Radio. On 1st November she arrived at Casablanca having averaged 4.5 knots for the passage. Whatever problems had arisen in the engine room, apparently the combined failure of both main and auxiliary machinery, and only superhuman efforts of her engineers could have got her to her destination, but that was as far as she ever managed under her own power. On 1st December she left Casablanca under tow and anchored in the Clyde in Fairlie Roads nine days later. On 18th December she dragged her anchors in a gale but was re-anchored three days later. She dragged again on 28th January 1950 and was towed to the more sheltered waters of the Holy Loch three days later and moored to a buoy, where she remained for the next ten weeks pending a decision on her future. The crew must have been paid off on her earlier arrival in Fairlie Roads.

By the spring of 1950 the Clunies company had been involved with the *Marianne Clunies* for 16 months and she had brought them nothing but grief and expense without the satisfaction of earning a single bean in freight, a situation which the two-year old company could ill afford. On 8th April a gang of riggers was sent to the ship in preparation for unmooring and three days later the *Marianne* was towed back to Greenock and berthed in the James Watt Dock that evening where she lay for the next three months. One wonders if the MacLeod turbine was removed in that period, but there is no evidence of a shift to or from the appropriate crane. (James MacLeod died eight years later). What is certain is that she was to pass to German owners who were then anxious to obtain whatever tonnage could be made available. The Clunies management arranged for

the departure of the ship under her existing name on the forenoon of 15th July, connection was made to a tug by midday when the local riggers landed and towage began to Bremerhaven where safe arrival was recorded six days later, the ship having averaged 6.5 knots for the passage. D. Oltmann of Bremen were relative newcomers to foreign-going ships but arranged the removal of all existing machinery and boilers and their replacement by a 12-cylinder MAN diesel built in 1945 for some other purpose. In September the *Marianne* was renamed *Ansgaritor* under which she traded successfully for another nine years until broken up in Holland at the grand old age of 44.

The *Alpha Zambesi*

During the ill-found voyage of the *Marianne Clunies* to Casablanca, another ship came under Clunies' management although not conforming to their nomenclature. In 1947 when the grain ship aircraft carriers were being sold off, the *Empire Macrae* was purchased by a newcomer to shipping entitled the Alpha South African Steamship Co. Ltd. of Durban, was placed under the management of Moller Line S.A. (Pty) Ltd., also of Durban, and renamed *Alpha Zambesi*. As such this ship continued to trade to eastern Canada and presumably still carried her flight deck. From the end of the war to June 1947 as *Empire Macrae* she carried 16 grain cargoes from either Montreal or Halifax to Liverpool, except one from Portland, Maine, and another from Baltimore to Hamburg.

As *Alpha Zambesi* under South African owners she carried another 19 grain cargoes from eastern Canada into Liverpool. On 6th March 1948 she was towed into Liverpool with four tugs due to steering gear failure, and on 3rd October that same year grounded in the St Lawrence but was refloated and returned to Montreal for repairs before resuming her homeward voyage two weeks later. After discharge in Liverpool in August 1949 there was a fire on board and it was at this time that ownership transferred to Motor Lines Ltd. of Gourock while management was placed with Clunies. A clue to the ownership of Motor Lines is that the managing owner recorded in registration documents

Empire Macrae. [J. and M. Clarkson collection]

By the summer of 1948, *Empire Macrae* had been renamed *Alpha Zambesi* and had embarked on a peacetime career carrying grain, but little had changed except the name. *[Mrs Margaret Johnstone]*

was Ian C. Caldwell, presumably of the engineers Caldwell Brothers (Marine) Ltd.

Without change of name, *Alpha Zambesi* left Liverpool on 20th November 1949 and berthed in the Great Harbour of Greenock two days later, where she was to remain for the next 11 months presumably having the flight deck removed and replaced by a modern superstructure as was then being fitted to *Doris Clunies* in the adjacent James Watt Dock and which was completed six months later.

Alpha Zambesi vacated her Greenock berth for eight days in the Garvel Drydock during September 1950 and sailed on 12th October for Hamburg, where she loaded cement for Buenos Aires and returned with iron ore from Pepel to Glasgow on 7th January 1951. Further trading that year began with two cargoes from Galveston: one each to Genoa and London. This was followed by grain cargoes, one from Portland, Maine, to Brake and four from Montreal; of which two were to Liverpool and one each to Antwerp and London. When outward bound from Liverpool in October 1951 she suffered heavy weather damage and steering gear failure but was repaired and reached Montreal safely after a lengthy passage of 16 days rather than the customary ten days. On returning to the Thames on the London voyage on 26th November 1951 Clunies' management ceased, Motor Lines' having transferred to a London address. This left only *Doris Clunies* in the fleet.

Final Clunies voyages

Having suffered the grievous loss of *James Clunies* in April 1949 and the lamentable disposal of *Marianne Clunies* in July 1953, the owners must have been considering their future when *Doris Clunies* had just begun her second voyage after conversion and *Margaret Clunies* was shortly due to arrive home from the Far East

During 1950 *Margaret Clunies* traded worldwide, going out initially from Hull to Karachi, where she was in collision and was detained two weeks for repairs, but then loaded in Bombay for Singapore and Hong Kong, returning from Taku Bar and similar ports to London, Rotterdam and Copenhagen, followed by a short trip from Finland to Barry. Her next and final voyage as a Clunies' ship was from Middlesbrough to Tripoli in the Lebanon, returning from Alexandria to Liverpool and Glasgow, arriving 11th January 1951, by which date the vessel had been sold to Turnbull Scott and Co. who took ownership in Glasgow with a change of name to *Waynegate*.

Doris Clunies, the first of the fleet, also proved to be the last. After acting as a grain store in the James Watt Dock, she discharged in Glasgow at the end of November 1949, then returned to Greenock for six months conversion from aircraft carrier to general tramp, berthing in the James Watt Dock on 5th December.

With the conversion work largely complete, *Doris Clunies* moved into the Garvel Drydock on 25th April 1950 for six days' survey, cleaning and painting, before returning to the James Watt Dock for a further four weeks to prepare for her first voyage without the encumbrance of the flight deck structure and sporting a modern bridge and funnel. She undocked at midday on 30th May, adjusted compasses, ran a short trial, landed Johnston and eight Caldwells' engineers at 17.30 and immediately proceeded to Montreal to load for London. It proved to be the final departure of a Clunies' owned ship from Greenock.

The remaining voyages of *Doris Clunies* in 1950 were from Galveston and Wilmington, North Carolina, to Amsterdam, Churchill to Dublin and New Orleans to Hamburg. For her 1951 voyages, by which time she was the sole unit of the fleet, *Doris Clunies* loaded at Antwerp on charter via Panama to New Plymouth, Wellington and Napier in New Zealand. She then proceeded to Geelong and loaded grain for Hull via Suez, arriving home on 10th August 1951. The *Doris* then moved to Rotterdam and in September was renamed *Sunrover* for a time charter to Saguenay Terminals Ltd. of Montreal. That company had expanded from one to ten ships since 1945, all under the Canadian flag, and reached their zenith in 1955 with 12 ships but then changed to British registry. *Sunrover* was one of 61 ships they chartered to operate their occasional tramping but mainly cargo liner service from east coast Canadian ports to the UK/Continent, thence to the Caribbean where they loaded bauxite from the Demerara River for the Saguenay River terminal adjacent to the St. Lawrence. In 1953, management of *Sunrover* passed to Dracoulis Ltd. of London but the Doris Steamship Co. Ltd. retained ownership of the ship until 1959, although it seems unlikely the Johnston family were involved beyond 1953.

Thus ended the bold and enterprising attempt by the Clunies Company at ship owning and ship management in the immediate post-war period, involving five ships and lasting just six years. Had the company not suffered the combined loss of the *James Clunies* and machinery failure of the *Marianne Clunies*, matters might well have turned out very differently.

The colour scheme adopted by Clunies was simple if unremarkable: black hulls and funnels on the *James* and *Margaret Clunies* but improved to buff coloured funnels on the two later conversions. Although berthage in Greenock was hardly ever visible to the general public who were therefore quite unaware of the Clunies company and its ships, those who worked on the waterfront in those now distant days, and certainly the nine crews who were engaged on their ships from that port, would recall the Clunies' (or rather the Johnstons') endeavours very well indeed.

Fleet list

1. DORIS CLUNIES/SUNROVER 1947-1953
O.N. 169508 8,252g 5,330n
429.5 x 57.9 x 35.3 feet
Burmeister & Wain-type oil engine 4SCSA 6-cyl. by J.G. Kincaid and Co. Ltd., Greenock; 12.5 knots.
12.10.1943: Launched by Lithgows Ltd., Port Glasgow (Yard No. 993).
22.12.1943: Completed for the Ministry of War Transport (Hain Steamship Co. Ltd., London, managers) as the merchant aircraft carrier EMPIRE MACCALLUM.
1.10.1947: Acquired by the Doris Steamship Co. Ltd. (Clunies Shipping Company, managers), Greenock.
12.1947: Renamed DORIS CLUNIES.
9.1951: Renamed SUNROVER.
1953: Managers became Dracoulis Ltd., London.

1957: Renamed EUDOXIA.
1959: Sold to the Phorkyss Shipping Corporation, Panama (Dracoulis Ltd., London, managers) and renamed PHORKYSS under the Lebanese flag.

1959: Transferred to the Greek flag.
28.5.1960: Laid up on the River Blackwater, Essex.
Prior to 8.11.1960: Arrived at Osaka.
10.11.1960: Breaking up began at Sakai.

Empire Maccallum after renaming *Doris Clunies*, but before major conversion work had been carried out. Note what is presumably a temporary uptake (upper).
Doris Clunies was photographed in Dublin Bay on 1st October 1950 bringing a cargo of grain from Churchill following conversion (lower). After removal of the flight deck the owner had a free hand in erecting superstructure, and her appearance was individualistic, to say the least. Note that she has three hatches abaft her superstructure. She is seen again as *Eudoxia* at Cape Town after sale of ship and company to Dracoulis Ltd. (opposite top). *[Mrs Margaret Johnstone; R.J. Scott/Pat Sweeney collection; Ships in Focus]*

2. JAMES CLUNIES 1947-1949

O.N. 181785 7,850g 5,790n
447.8 x 56.2 x 35.6 feet
T. 3-cyl. by Glenfield and Kennedy Ltd.,
Kilmarnock; 541 NHP, 2,550 BHP, 12 knots.
2.11.1944: Launched by William Gray and
Co. Ltd., West Hartlepool (Yard No. 1171).

1.1945: Completed for the Royal Navy as
the aircraft maintenance ship CUILLIN
SOUND.
14.11.1947: Registered in the ownership of
the Margareta Steamship Co. Ltd. (Clunies
Shipping Company, managers), Greenock as
JAMES CLUNIES.

7.1948: Conversion to a cargo ship
completed.
21.4.1949: Wrecked 1½ miles and 347
degrees from Punta Mogotes, Argentina
whilst on a voyage from Bahia Blanca to
Italy with a cargo of grain.
13.7.1949: Register closed.

James Clunies at Amsterdam on 18th February 1949 loading coal for Buenos Aires before her last fateful voyage. *[Foto-Technisch Bureau Van Es/ Mrs Margaret Johnstone]*

3. MARGARET CLUNIES 1948-1951

O.N. 181786 7,416g 5,327n
447.8 x 56.3 x35.6 feet
T.3-cyl. by Duncan Stewart and Co. Ltd.,
Glasgow; 10 knots.
10.7.1944: Launched by Bartram and Sons
Ltd., Sunderland (Yard No. 301).
Completed for The Admiralty as the
maintenance ship MULLION COVE
(pennant number F.186).
She had been laid down as the 'C' type
cargo ship EMPIRE PENANG.
1948: Acquired by the Margareta Steamship
Co. Ltd. (Clunies Shipping Company,
managers), Greenock and renamed
MARGARET CLUNIES.
7.1948: Conversion to a cargo ship
completed.

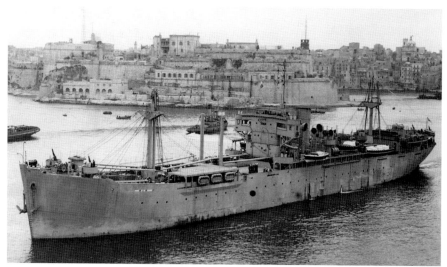

1951: Sold to the Turnbull Scott
Shipping Co. Ltd. (Turnbull, Scott and
Co., managers), London and renamed
WAYNEGATE.
1961: Sold to Pacifico Compania Naviera
S.A., Panama (Harry Hadjipateras Brothers,
Piraeus, Greece) and renamed KATINGO
under the Greek flag.
1964: Sold to Philippine President Lines
Inc., Manila, Philippines and renamed
PRESIDENT MAGSAYSAY.
1968: Renamed MAGSAYSAY.
19.7.1968: Damaged by fire in engine room
off south west Korea in position 34.48 north
by 125.51 east whilst on a voyage from
the Philippines to Inchon with a cargo of
logs. Abandoned, but reboarded and fire
extinguished the next day. Later declared a
constructive total loss.
30.12.1968: Delivered to Busan, Korea to
be broken up by Kyong Nam Products Co.

Three stages in a career: the
maintenance ship *Mullion Cove* at
Malta (top); as *Margaret Clunies*
loading in a US port (middle) and
as *Waynegate* in the Mersey during

Turnbull Scott ownership (bottom).
[J. and M. Clarkson collection;
National Maritime Museum, P23349;
B. and A. Feilden/J. and M. Clarkson]

4. MARIANNE CLUNIES 1949-1950

O.N.168195 5,880g 3,586n

423.8 x 54.2 x 27.7 feet

Geared steam turbine by General Electric Company, Schenectady, New York, USA.

1949: Geared steam turbine by the Macleod Steam Turbine Co. Ltd. Glasgow and made in 1939 by Bellis and Morcom Ltd., Birmingham; 2,500 SHP, 8.5 knots.

1950: Oil engine 4SCSA 12-cyl. made in 1945 by Maschinenbau Augsburg-Nürnberg A.G., Augsburg, Germany.

6.1918: Completed by Northwest Steel Company, Portland, Oregon, USA for the United States Shipping Board, Washington DC, USA as WESTERN OCEAN.

1937: Transferred to the United States Maritime Commission, Washington DC.

26.6.1941: Registered in the ownership of the Ministry of War Transport, London (G. Heyn and Sons Ltd., Belfast, managers) and renamed EMPIRE OPOSSUM.

20.3.1946: Owners became the Ministry of War Transport, London.

13.12.1948: Acquired by the James Steamship Co. Ltd. (Clunies Shipping Company, managers), Greenock and subsequently re-engined.

30.8.1949: Renamed MARIANNE CLUNIES.

13.7.1950: Register closed on sale to D. Oltmann (Unterweser Reederei A.G., managers), Bremen, West Germany, subsequently renamed ANSGARITOR and re-engined.

15.7.1950: Left the Clyde for Bremen in tow of the motor tug WOTAN.

1951: Transferred to Schlüssel Reed D. Oltmann, Bremen.

27.10.1958: During a voyage from Narvik to Rotterdam touched ground.

30.10.1958: Arrived at Rotterdam and subsequently laid up.

3.1959: Sold to Dutch breakers and broken up at Krimpen a/d Ijsel.

Marianne Clunies on trials, photographed by Graham Langmuir as she approached Loch Long on 12th September 1949. She has been modernised and the appearance of her superstructure belies her 31 years (top). *[Roy Fenton collection]*

The profile of *Marianne Clunies* changed again when as the German *Ansgaritor* she was given her third engine (middle and bottom). *[J. and M. Clarkson; World Ship Society Ltd.]*

5. ALPHA ZAMBESI 1949-1951

O.N. 169507 8,252g 5,330n
444.7 x 57.9 35.3 feet
Burmeister & Wain-type oil engine 4SCSA
6-cyl. by J.G. Kincaid and Co. Ltd.,
Greenock; 255 NHP, 3,300 BHP, 4,075 IHP,
12 knots.
21.6.1943: Launched by Lithgows, Ltd.,
Port Glasgow (Yard No. 992).
23.9.1943: Registered in the ownership
of the Ministry of War Transport (Hain
Steamship Co. Ltd., managers), London
as the merchant aircraft carrier EMPIRE
MACRAE.
27.1.1947: Sold to Moller Line Ltd.,
London.
21.5.1947: Transferred to the Alpha South
African Steamship Co. Ltd. (Moller Line
S.A. (Pty.) Ltd.), Durban, South Africa.
30.6.1947: Renamed ALPHA ZAMBESI.
10.11.1949: Transferred to Moller Line Ltd.,
Hong Kong.
15.11.1949: Acquired by Motor Lines Ltd.,
Gourock (Clunies Shipping Company,
Greenock, managers).
27.6.1951: Owners now based in London.
26.11.1951: Management ceased.
26.2.1954: Sold to Westport Shipping Co.
Ltd. (Lennart S. Waldemar, manager),
London.
2.10.1954: Register closed on sale to
Skibs A/S Vilhelm Torkildsens Rederi &
Dampskip A/S Flint (Vilhelm Torkildsen,
manager), Bergen, Norway and renamed
TOBON.
1960: Sold to Dampskip A/S Flint (Willy
Kubon, manager), Bergen.
1967: Sold to Agia Paraskevi Corporation,
Panama (Pontikos Shipping Agencies (E.
Pontikos), Piraeus, Greece) and renamed
DESPINA P under the Greek flag.
Prior to 7.4.1971: Arrived Kaohsiung.
2.5.1971: Breaking up began by the Chi
Shun Hwa Steel and Iron Works Company.
5.6.1971: Work completed.

Rebuilding *Alpha Zambesi* as a conventional freighter in 1949/1950 gave her an appearance similar to that of *Doris Clunies*, with six pairs of kingposts and a box-like bridge structure carrying an odd erection on top. The photographs show her under three different names and colour schemes, as first rebuilt as *Alpha Zambesi* (top), as the Norwegian *Tobon* (middle), and as the unkempt, Greek-owned *Despina P* (bottom by Airfoto, Malacca). *[All J. and M. Clarkson collection]*

MERCHANT AIRCRAFT CARRIERS - GRAIN SHIPS

Roy Fenton

The six grain ship/aircraft carriers, two of which were referred to in the accompanying Clunies history and fleet list, were a remarkably successful amalgamation of two conflicting design requirements. Fortunately, those who conceived and helped execute the designs recorded full and fairly frank accounts of their work.

The merchant aircraft carrier (MAC) was conceived as a way of closing the air gap in mid-Atlantic which could not be covered by shore-based aircraft. They were something of a stop-gap, as at the time they were designed a programme of building naval auxiliary carriers was getting under way in the USA and the UK. Unlike their predecessors, the catapult-aircraft merchant ships, the MACs had the advantage of not losing an aircraft after its mission, nor of guaranteeing the pilot a dunking in the cold North Atlantic.

The conversion of merchant ships into auxiliary aircraft carriers had begun with the former German motor vessel *Hannover* which became HMS *Audacity*. Although a very early war loss, this vessel showed the usefulness and practicability of the concept in protecting convoys. Unlike this commissioned ship, the merchant aircraft carriers would fly the Red Ensign, and were sailed by merchant navy officers and men, with the Royal Navy providing the aircrew and support staff. Like so many aspects of their design, this was a compromise between the urgent requirement to provide convoys with air cover and the pressing need for the carrying capacity of as many cargo ships as possible.

The need to fit a flight deck ruled out conventional deck-mounted cargo gear and hatches, and meant that the ships could handle only cargo which could be sucked or pumped out, restricting them to carrying grain or oil. The tanker conversions (nine) and new builds (two) were, in fact, the more numerous, but this article concentrates on

the six grain ships built in three groups of two each at the Burntisland, Lithgow and Denny yards.

Compromises, compromises

When the idea of a merchant aircraft carrier was first put forward, the air staff at the Admiralty insisted that the minimum speed acceptable was 15 knots, pointing out that no aircraft carrier had been built with a design speed less than 19 knots (in fact, HMS *Audacity* had a speed of 15 knots). The Admiralty Merchant Shipbuilding Department, responsible for all wartime merchant ship production, replied that 15-knot ships were simply not available, as all were wanted for carrying food. Reluctantly the Air Staff agreed to 11-knot ships, but expressed doubts as to whether they would be much use as carriers. To give a margin of power to manoeuvre into take-off and landing positions and rejoin a convoy afterwards required more powerful engines than the 2,500 BHP diesels usual for wartime standard cargo ships, and 3,300 BHP was specified, giving about 12½ knots. All the MACs, both dry cargo and tanker, were diesel-driven, as the smoke from a steam engine's boiler would have caused difficulties. The diesel exhaust was ejected horizontally from trunks under the flight deck, a pair being fitted to allow the smoke to be diverted to whichever was the lee side during flying operations.

The next compromise was over size. Air Staff wanted a flight deck no less than 490 feet long and 62 feet wide, with a hangar capable of housing six aircraft. Again they were told that what they could have was determined by the shipyard berths then available, and they agreed – although apparently not unanimously – to a minimum flight deck length of 390 feet. In the grain ships, but not the tankers, a hangar was installed capable of taking four Fairey Swordfish aircraft with folded wings. Careful

On 8th March 1940, the Royal Navy captured Norddeutscher Lloyd's *Hannover* (5,537/1939) off Central America. Initially renamed *Sinbad*, in 1941 the prize was rebuilt and entered service as the merchant aircraft carrier *Empire Audacity* in September of that year. Her career was tragically short: torpedoed by U 751 on 21st December 1941 whilst escorting convoy HG.76. She had, however, proven the value of such conversions in convoy protection. *[J. and M. Clarkson collection]*

attention was paid to ventilation, heating, lighting and fire-fighting equipment in the hangar, and a five-ton lift installed capable of moving a loaded plane to flight deck level in 50 seconds. The Air Staff would have liked storage facilities for ammunition and aviation spirit to conform to naval requirements and be disposed away from the ships' sides and below the waterline, but the only space available was alongside the hangar.

At what appeared to one of those involved as 'innumerable' meetings (others recall there were just three) in the late spring of 1942, agreement was hammered out over other matters concerning how much naval equipment the ships would carry. Fitting of ASDIC was strongly advocated, on the grounds that detecting a submarine would allow evasive action to be taken. But fitting ASDIC complicated building, and as this would delay completion it was dropped. In contrast, radar was fitted as it would not delay work, although the need for radar operators increased

the ship's complement. A compromise was reached over night flying equipment, thought essential as U-boat attacks often occurred during darkness. Full deck lighting would delay building, and there was a shortage of shipyard electricians to fit it, so simple emergency deck lighting was installed, and in service proved quite adequate.

Completion and service

The order for the first grain carrier was placed with the Burntisland Shipbuilding Co Ltd. in June 1942, a date itself quite impressive as planning had only got going in May. The detailed design work was shared with the other two yards involved, as none of the three had any experience of naval work. The original plan was to complete six at intervals between April 1943 and March 1944. However, although the *Empire MacAlpine* was ready in April 1943 following flying trials in the Clyde, the others were late, largely it seems due to delayed delivery of the aircraft

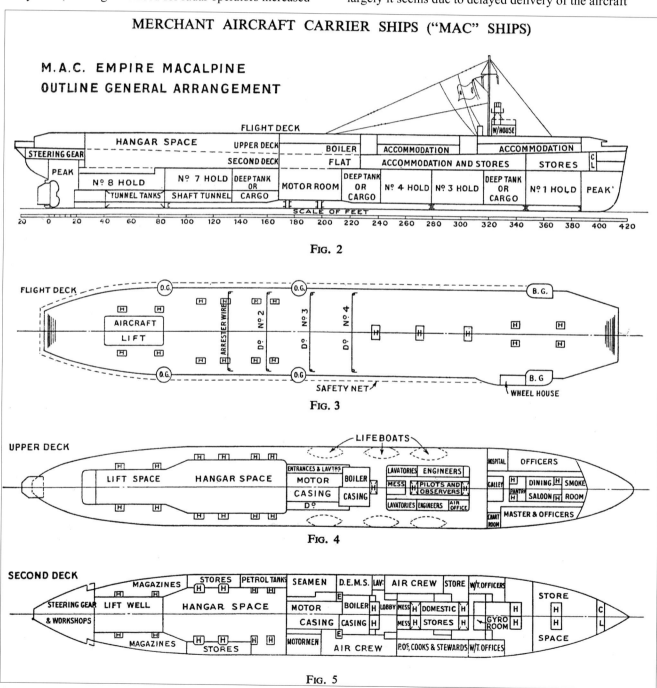

General arrangement drawing of the *Empire MacAlpine*. As each of the three yards in the building programme used their standard hull, there were detailed variations between the three groups of MAC ships, with overall length varying by as much as 12 feet.

elevator and arrester gear, the former at least coming from the USA. An illustration of the extra work involved above and beyond the construction of a normal merchant ship was the increase of 25% in cost, partly due to the 20% extra steelwork required for the flight deck and hangar, but also involving accommodation for the combined mercantile and naval crew which totalled over 120. Perhaps surprisingly, given the size of the hangar, cargo capacity was reduced by only 28% compared with a conventional cargo ship of comparable size. On her maiden voyage, the *Empire MacAlpine* loaded a grain cargo in three days with no particular difficulty and was unloaded at Liverpool in less than 24 hours.

The pessimists at the Admiralty had doubts about whether a merchant navy crew could operate aircraft carriers. By all accounts this does not seem to have been a problem, the future masters being sent on courses at the Western Approaches Tactical School and in Royal Navy carriers. At one stage of the design process it was considered necessary to have separate messes for the two types of officer, but this did not happen. It is reported that the merchant navy and Fleet Air Arm men got along very well, despite considerable differences in both pay and accommodation which favoured the former. On occasions merchant navy officers went up in the Swordfishes as unofficial observers!

The Air Staff's reservations about operating aircraft from such short flight decks were equally unfounded. Experience showed that against a wind of 25 to 30 knots a loaded aircraft could take off in 360 feet. Some high rates of launchings were achieved; on one occasion three aircraft were dispatched in just 16 seconds and landed again in 42 seconds. There were four arrester wires stretched transversely across the after 90 feet of deck, but with no crash barrier. During flying trials it was found that all aircraft picked up either the first or the second wire.

The MAC ships were essentially defensive in concept, and were soon somewhat eclipsed by the arrival of faster and better-equipped escort carriers which flew the White Ensign. They are reckoned to have sunk at least one U-boat, and their aircrafts' patrols may well have foiled

Empire Macalpine in dry dock at Cammell Laird and Co. Ltd., Birkenhead on 10th July 1943. *[Imperial War Museum A 18007]*

many more attacks on convoys. Their effect on morale of the merchant navy was excellent. At one convoy conference the Naval Control Service Officer was asked if there was to be a MAC ship present. When he replied in the affirmative, the 50 or so masters present spontaneously applauded. The apparently almost impossible task of designing a ship which could carry a substantial cargo of grain or oil and could function successfully as an aircraft carrier had been achieved.

Empire Macalpine. [Imperial War Museum FL 10700]

Merchant aircraft carrier *Empire Macalpine* with four Fairey Swordfish Mark IIs of No. 836 Naval Air Squadron on the flight deck. *[Imperial War Museum HU 64545]*

Empire Macalpine at sea. The photographs on this page were taken during landing trials 7-10th May 1943. *[Ben Line Archives]*

Mr Campbell, Chief Officer of *Empire Macalpine*, giving an official welcome to Lieutenant R. W. Slater, DSC, RN, the first pilot to land a naval aircraft on a merchant ship on 7th May 1943. *[Imperial War Museum A 17067]*

Empire Macalpine with a Fairey Swordfish about to land showing the arrester gear (middle right), and bringing a Swordfish on to the deck from the hanger below (bottom). *[Imperial War Museum A 17068; Ben Line Archives]*

1. EMPIRE MACALPINE 1943-1946

O.N. 123106   7,954g 5,255n
417.1 x 57.0 x 33.7 feet
4-cyl. 2SCSA oil engine by William Doxford and Sons Ltd., Sunderland; 3,400 BHP; 12.5 knots.

11.8.1942: Keel laid.

23.12.1942: Launched by Burntisland Shipbuilding Co. Ltd., Burntisland (Yard No. 268).

14.4.1943: Registered at Burntisland in the ownership of the Ministry of War Transport, London as the merchant aircraft carrier EMPIRE MACALPINE.

21.4.1943: Trials completed and handed over to William Thomson and Co., Leith as managers.

3.1946: Owners became the Ministry of Transport, London.

12.1946: Sold to McCowen and Gross Ltd., London who had her converted to a conventional cargo ship.

10.1947: Renamed DERRYNANE.

11.1951: Transferred to the Power Steam Ship Co. Ltd. (McCowen and Gross Ltd. and later O. Gross and Sons Ltd., managers), London and renamed HUNTSBROOK.

19.7.1959: Laid-up in the River Blackwater, Essex.

10.1959: Sold to South Breeze Navigation Co. Ltd. (John Manners and Co. Ltd., managers), Hong Kong and renamed SUVA BREEZE.

1965: Transferred to San Fernando Steam Ship Co. S.A., Panama (John Manners and Co. Ltd., Hong Kong, managers), and renamed DJATINGALEH.

1966: Renamed SAN ERNESTO.

1967: Managers became Jaguar Shipping Corporation (I. Wang), Hong Kong.

1968: Sold to Compania Nueva del Oriente S.A., Panama (Jaguar Shipping Corporation (I. Wang), Hong Kong) and renamed PACIFIC ENDEAVOUR.

21.2.1970: Arrived at Hong Kong for breaking up by Wise Investment Co. Ltd.

Officially captioned 'Discharging grain from a MAC ship at a north-west port', this is almost certainly *Empire Macalpine* and undoubtedly Liverpool (top). She is seen following conversion in the Thames as *Derrynane* (middle) and finally *Huntsbrook* (bottom) *[V.H. Young collection; W.H. Brown/Roy Fenton collection; Roy Fenton collection]*

EMPIRE MACANDREW 1943-1946

O.N. 168767 7,952g 5,219n
448.5 x 56.3 x 25.2 feet
4SCSA 6-cyl. Burmeister & Wain-type
oil engine by J.G. Kincaid and Co. Ltd.,
Greenock; 3,300 BHP, 12 knots.
3.5.1943: Launched by William Denny and
Brothers Ltd., Dumbarton (Yard No. 1370)
for the Ministry of War Transport, London
as the merchant aircraft carrier EMPIRE
MACANDREW.
7.7.1943: Completed, the Hain Steamship
Co. Ltd., London appointed managers.
23.10.1946: Sold to McCowen and Gross
Ltd., London, later converted to a cargo ship
at Liverpool and renamed DERRYHEEN
(5,308g 2,956n).
1951: Sold to the Lyle Shipping Co. Ltd.,
Glasgow and renamed CAPE GRAFTON.
1963: Sold to Patricia Compania Naviera
S.A., Panama (Chios Navigation Co. Ltd.,
London) and renamed PATRICIA.
1968: Sold to Pomos Shipping Co. Ltd.,
Nicosia, Cyprus (Chios Navigation Co. Ltd.,
London).
1970: Sold to the China National Machinery
Import and Export Corporation.
4.10.1970: Delivered to Hsinkiang, China to
be broken up.

Empire MacAndrew (top) became the
conventional cargo ship as *Derryheen*
(middle). McCowen and Gross Ltd.
had two of these MAC ships, and
the conversions produced a similar
appearance. *Derryheen* was sold to
Lyle Shipping in 1951 and was renamed
Cape Grafton (bottom). *[J. and M.
Clarkson collection; Ships in Focus;
FotoFlite/J. and M. Clarkson collection]*

3. EMPIRE MACRAE
see Clunies fleet list.

4. EMPIRE MACCALLUM
see Clunies fleet list.

5. EMPIRE MACKENDRICK 1944-1946
O.N. 123108 7,933g 5,106n
417.1 x 57.0 x 35.1 feet
4SCSA 6-cyl. oil engine by J. G. Kincaid and
Co. Ltd., Greenock; 3,300 BHP, 12 knots.
29.9.1943: Launched by Burntisland
Shipbuilding Co. Ltd., Burntisland (Yard
No. 277) for the Ministry of War Transport,
London as the merchant aircraft carrier
EMPIRE MACKENDRICK.
12.1943: Completed, William Thomson and
Co. appointed managers and registered at
Burntisland.
3.1946: Owners became the Ministry of
Transport, London.
12.1946: Sold to Mediterranean and Atlantic
Lines Ltd. (Goulandris Brothers Ltd.,
managers), London.
12.1947: Renamed GRANPOND.
26.6.1949: Arrived at Barrow and laid-up.
1.1951: Transferred to Compania Maritima
del Este S.A., Panama (Goulandris Brothers
(Hellas) Ltd., Piraeus) and renamed
CONDOR.
22.2.1951: Arrived in tow at Hamburg for
conversion to a conventional merchant ship.
1953: Transferred to Societa Armadora del
Norte S.A., Panama (Goulandris Brothers
(Hellas) Ltd., Piraeus).
1.1955: Sold to Turnbull, Scott Shipping Co.
Ltd. (Turnbull, Scott and Co. Ltd., managers),
London and renamed SALTERSGATE.

Empire Macrae when new. Note the small size of the bridge. *[Roy Fenton Collection]*

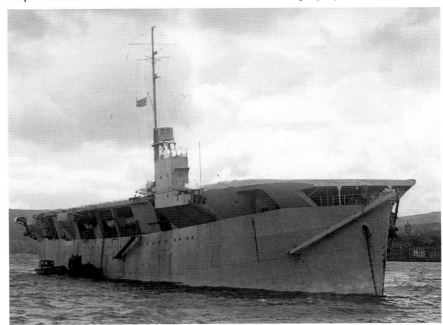

Giving the MAC ships 'Empire' names beginning *Mac* was a nice touch, as was naming one *Empire Mackendrick* (middle) after the captain of the ill-fated pioneer conversion

Empire Audacity. She is seen in an unconverted state as *Granpond* in March 1949 (above) before she was laid up at Barrow. Note the smoke from her exhaust. As *Basil Levski*

the ship had eight years of enforced idleness in the Great Bitter Lakes.
[Imperial War Museum, A18029; Cliff Parsons/Roy Fenton collection]

24.12.1956: Arrived at Grangemouth.
1.1957: Sold to Navigation Maritime Bulgare, Varna, Bulgaria and renamed BASIL LEVSKI.
5.6.1967: Trapped in Great Bitter Lake, Suez Canal, on the outbreak of Arab-Israel War.
16.5.1975: Arrived at Port Said, Egypt, following the re-opening of the Suez Canal.
22.7.1975: Arrived in tow at Split, Yugoslavia for breaking up by Brodospas.

6. EMPIRE MACDERMOTT 1944-1947
O.N. 169407 7,952g 5,224n
448.5 x 56.3 x 34.2 feet

4SCSA 6-cyl. Burmeister & Wain-type oil engine by J.G. Kincaid and Co. Ltd., Greenock; 3,300 BHP, 12 knots.
24.1.1944: Launched by William Denny and Brothers Ltd., Dumbarton (Yard No. 1378) for the Ministry of War Transport, London as the merchant aircraft carrier EMPIRE MACDERMOTT.
3.1944: Completed, the Hain Steamship Co. Ltd., London appointed managers.
1947: Sold to Buries Markes Ltd., London.
1948: Converted to a merchant ship by D. and W. Henderson Ltd., Glasgow and renamed LA CUMBRE (7,371g 4,352n).

11.1958: Sold to Canero Compania Naviera S.A., Panama (Lyras Brothers Ltd., London) for £215,000 and renamed PARNON under the Greek flag.
1969: Sold to Southern Shipping and Enterprises Ltd. (Yick Fung Shipping and Enterprises Co. Ltd.), Hong Kong and renamed STARLIGHT under the Somali flag.
1975: Transferred to China Ocean Shipping Company, Beijing, China.
1992: Deleted from 'Lloyd's Register' as continued existence in doubt.

La Cumbre, the former Empire MacDermott, shows a further variation on the conversion, with a forecastle, long derricks, a more shapely funnel and extensive superstructure trunked around the third hatch. Although the date of her demise is unknown, she was almost certainly the longest-lived of the MAC grain ships. [W.T. Hubbard/Roy Fenton collection]

PUTTING THE RECORD STRAIGHT

Letters, additions, amendments and photographs relating to features in any issues of 'Record' are welcomed. Communications by e-mail are quite acceptable, but senders are asked to include their postal address. Letters may be lightly edited. Correspondence on subjects in multipart articles is usually held over until the series has been completed.

The editors would deem it a great kindness if readers submitting letters for this column would as far as possible follow our current editorial style, and in particular put names of ships into upper and lower case italics and not capitals.

***Timaru Star's* accommodation**
Regarding the comments in 'Record' 42 in respect of *Tuscan Star*, when she arrived at Auckland on 9th June 1947 on her first visit to New Zealand, under the command of Captain Gavin C. Goudie, it was reported that she had accommodation for 96 passengers. Blue Star had taken over her management from P&O in January 1947.

Another report when she returned to Dunedin as *Timaru Star* in June 1949 states that following her earlier visit in November 1948 she had her wartime accommodation removed and new accommodation built for 12 passengers. Altogether the vessel lay in dry dock on the Tyne for about five months.

The Blue Star Line Superintendent's Department's capacity plan dated 21st April 1949 shows accommodation for only 12 passengers, with the bridge deck now having 53,965 cubic feet of cargo space (capacity for about 2,400 bales of wool). She also had the extended funnel when this plan was made.

The image of *Timaru Star* on page 57 of 'Record' 41 was taken as she left Dunedin for Lyttelton on 5th November 1948.
IAN FARQUHAR, RD2, Dunedin, New Zealand
Thanks also to Robert Langlois for correspondence about this ship. His research confirms Alan Mallett's view, expressed on page 124 of 'Record' 42, that as Empire Clarendon *she was built to a Union-Castle design. Ed.*

More under the Star and Crescent

I have discovered two further British-built ships owned in Pakistan and which I omitted in my series of articles 'Under the Star and Crescent: British-built Ships owned in Pakistan' in 'Record' 34 to 36. They were the *Mansoor* (4,512/1940) and the *Mustansir* (5,627/1949), both owned by Gulf Steamships Co. Ltd., which was controlled by Fakhruddin Millwalla and family of Karachi. The *Mansoor* was bought in 1958 and was previously the *Cape Wrath* of Lyle Shipping Co. Ltd. of Glasgow, and had been built by Lithgows of Port Glasgow. She served Gulf until 1966 when she was broken up at Karachi. The *Mustansir* was acquired in 1959 and had been built as the *Irish Cedar* for Irish Shipping Ltd., Dublin, by William Gray at West Hartlepool, and traded for Gulf until sold for demolition at Karachi in 1971.

Some further information has come to light about the Pakistan Government-owned National Shipping Corporation (NSC), which inaugurated their first regular liner service to Britain and North Europe on 15th March 1964, using chartered ships. The NSC's first ship was the *Rupsa*, ex- *La Falda* of Buries Markes Ltd., which was acquired on 31st March 1964, and is featured on page 202 of 'Record' 36. By 1970-71, just before the Bangladesh War, the NSC fleet numbered 32 ships with a total deadweight of 343,757 tons.

PETER MYERS, 69 Westbank Park, Old Meldrum, Inverurie, Aberdeenshire, AB51 0DG

Ulimaroa aground again

Just to clear up some possible confusion regarding *Ulimaroa* ('Record' 41 page 64 and 42 page 128). According to 'Huddart Parker' by W.A. Laxon she went aground in the River Tay on 2nd December 1907 sustaining considerably damage and after repairs at Newcastle-on-Tyne she managed to go aground again after trials on 2nd January 1908. She was refloated undamaged on 4th January.

JOHN WOODLEY by e-mail

Two British-built ships sold to Gulf Steamships Co. Ltd. were the *Cape Wrath* (upper) which became *Mansoor* in 1958 and *Irish Cedar* (lower) which was renamed *Mustansir* in 1959. *[Ships in Focus; Fotoflite incorporating Skyfotos/J. and M. Clarkson collection]*

EVERY PICTURE TELLS A STORY

Araluen before lengthening. *[Ships in Focus]*

In the first issue of 'Record' an article on the Australind Steam Shipping Co. Ltd. included a photograph of the motor vessel *Araluen* (8,485/1958) taken in 1971. In his caption the editor noted that the extra hold forward of the superstructure compared with her predecessor *Ajana* (5,267/1950) unbalanced her profile. What the writer failed to realise was that the *Araluen* had been lengthened in 1966.

The article prompted Roy Metcalfe to forward the accompanying photographs, taken whilst *Araluen's* lengthening operation was underway at the Belfast yard of Harland and Wolfe Ltd. The bow section had been detached, but on floating out of dry dock it capsized. Roy recalls that the naval architects issued instructions for the foremast to

be removed to maintain stability, but these were ignored by the repair department to save time. Fortunately no-one was injured, although a couple of ship yard men ended up in the water. Roy thinks his photographs are probably unique, as the harbour police were keeping the press and television cameras at bay and preventing photography. An apprentice in the yard, Roy smuggled in a small camera and took the photographs whilst the police were not looking.

It took two weeks to right the fore end of the *Araluen* so that her lengthening could proceed. She remained in service with Australind until 1973, and then worked for Hong Kong owners as *Tai Shan* and *Rockferry* until demolished at Kaohsiung in 1982.

Roy Metcalfe's photographs of the mishap to the *Araluen* at Belfast in 1966.

BOSUN'S LOCKER

Sadly we have to start the Bosun's Locker with two obituaries which have kindly been compiled by Charles Waine.

Phillip N. Thomas

Phil Thomas's initial interest was aircraft and he joined the R.A.F. in 1942, training in Canada as a navigator/wireless operator. After the war he attended Glasgow University, obtaining an honours degree in electrical engineering and joined the textile company, J. and P. Coates. The retirement of the tug *George Brown* began his interest in steam tugs and he built up a library of information including a card index of the thousands of steam tugs built for British owners. He was a keen model maker and a leading member of his local model boat club. Reasoning that sale and purchase brokers probably kept plans and photos of the vessels they acted for, he approached McLarens and found a treasure trove of material dating back to the latter part of the nineteenth century. This and other material he located featured in the numerous articles he wrote for 'Model Boats' and 'Model Shipwright' for which he prepared plans suitable for model making, sometimes surveying the old tugs himself. This led him to write the definitive work 'British Steam Tugs', in 1984 and still in print today. On retirement he produced a similar work, 'British Ocean Tramps', published in 1992. Another of his interests was ship figureheads, and this led to the publication of 'British Figurehead and Ship Carvers' in 1995. Perhaps his most challenging project was his final work, 'Steamships 1835-1875 in Contemporary Records' published in 2008,

listing comprehensive details of almost 8,000 vessels. Phil was married with three children.

Richard J. Scott

Dick Scott became interested in the trading schooners and ketches visiting Dublin at an early age and was to sail on a number of them during his holidays, beginning with the *Brooklands* in 1945, the very last home trade schooner relying on sail alone. He became a close friend of Captain Tom Jewell of Appledore, Devon and made many voyages in the *Kathleen & May* ending when she was sold out of trade in 1960. He remained a keen sailor and for many years was a member of the Maritime Institute of Ireland. In 1981 he received the first special award of the Galway Hooker Association for services to traditional craft and his book 'The Galway Hookers' was first published in 1983. His lifelong interest in sail was coupled with a keen interest in photography, and his legacy is a superb collection of action photos aboard schooners and ketches at sea. These and his extensive collection of other photos and detailed histories of Irish schooners form the basis of the book 'Twilight of the Schooners' which he had just completed at the time of his death and which is to be published by Ships in Focus. A fitting tribute was paid to Dick on the morning of his funeral, 26th January 2008, when the *Kathleen & May* flew her red ensign at half mast. Dick was married with three children.

We send our condolences to the families and friends of both Phil and Dick.

Wincham on her building bertrh at Northwich and shortly after her launch on 15th July 1948. [Clive Guthrie collection]

Our next item could almost be described as another obituary. In the editorial for 'Record' 42, we singled out the Merseyside Maritime Museum for criticism, and it seems we are in good company, as 'Private Eye' for 15th May has also had a go at them. This is over the scrapping of the Weaver packet *Wincham*, which has been at the Museum since retiring in the 1970s. When she was slipped for inspection a surveyor became concerned about the state of some of her hull plates and condemned them. Her owners, the Wincham Preservation Society, could not afford the repairs and the *Wincham* was sold for demolition. The Preservation Society would normally have turned to the Friends of the Merseyside Maritime Museum for help, but Dr David Fleming, the Director of National Museums on Merseyside, had disbanded the Friend's organisation because it was critical of his policies. The new Museum of Liverpool, a pet scheme of Dr Fleming, is costing £72,000,000. The cost of repairing *Wincham* was estimated to be £40,000.

Wincham in the Manchester Ship Canal, approaching Eastham locks in 1972. *[J. and M. Clarkson]*

When laying out a book, be it 'Record' or one of our other publications, it is surprising how often a photograph reaches us just when it is too late. Such was the case with the photograph below of the *Wanganella*, formerly Elder Dempster's *Achimota*. In fact three arrived, one was already in the book having been submitted by another contributor, the second we used on the cover but there was nothing we could do with the third, one reproduced below, taken whilst she was being refitted. The same happened with the *Dolphin Shell* in 'Record' 42. We had difficulty finding good images to illustrate the article 'Shell's former sailing ship tankers' but soon after printing we were sent two fine images of her in the Brisbane River and these are reproduced overleaf. Thank you to Murray Robinson, co-author of 'A Tasman Trio', and to Warwick Foote, one time owner of the negatives from which these Shell photographs have been taken, who have kindly written the respective captions for us.

The *Wanganella*, formerly *Achimota*, under tow at Belfast in November 1932, most probably just after Harland and Wolff had repainted her in the colours of her new owner, Huddart Parker Ltd. of Australia. Completed to the order of Elder Dempster and Company Ltd in July 1931, she is being refitted for Huddart Parker's weekly service across the Tasman Sea between Sydney, Australia and Wellington, New Zealand. Note the platform in front of the bridge, rigged for shipyard carpenters who are extending the liner's wheelhouse. The story of the *Wanganella's* long and colourful life, along with that of her trans-Tasman consorts *Monowai* and *Awatea*, has just been published by Ships In Focus Publications in our new book 'A Tasman Trio : Wanganella - Awatea - Monowai' by Andrew Bell and Murray Robinson. See our contact details inside the front cover. *[Caption; Murray Robinson]*

These views of Shell's sailing ship tanker *Dolphin Shell* ('Record' 42) show her outward bound in the Brisbane River on a clear winter's day in the mid-1920s. Her almost brand-new appearance vessel suggests she had come down from the Far East for maintenance and painting in the South Brisbane Dry Dock. *Dolphin Shell* is entering the wide Hamilton Reach of the winding Brisbane River, which offers ship photographers a choice of locations from which the best views can be obtained in the prevailing seasons and weather conditions. The riverside houses in the upper photo are now obscured by boatyards and moorings. The tall structure to the left of the funnel in the lower shot is a chimney at a soap factory, which closed in the late 1930s.

The photographs were taken by William Sluce, a prolific ship photographer in Brisbane from about 1923 until the late1960s. His extensive negative collection was dispersed some years ago and is now held by shipping enthusiasts in the UK and New Zealand. His prints are in the possession of the Queensland Maritime Museum. *[Photos: V. H. Young and L. A. Sawyer, caption: Warwick Foote]*

Eight interesting photographs follow for which we have, at best, only partial details. We would welcome any further information, but when replying please quote the reference number printed in bold at the beginning of the caption.

43/03. There is a good chance that this unfortunate incident took place at Hull as the postcard was produced by Gledstone and Barnard of Hull. There is no date, but can anyone identify the paddle steamer and suggest when she sank?

43/04. The only clue in this photograph is what is possibly the Tower of Refuge on Conister Rock in Douglas Bay in the background. There is no cargo gear but there are a few passengers aft of the superstructure: is it a tender or a pilot boat?

43/01. Is this an early bulk carrier? The funnel bears the letters 'US' with underneath them a device shaped like a fob watch. The card was posted from Canada to the USA in 1929.

43/02. This card was published in the USA and shows a whaleback steamer, although when I first glanced at it I thought it was a ship which had broken in half! The letter 'S' on her funnel may offer a clue to her identity.

43/07. The tug is the *Iris*, but I have no name for the very British-looking three-masted topsail schooner. The view is familiar, but I have not been able to find where it was published. In the haze to the right is a Pacific Steam or Royal Mail liner.

43/08. Can anyone enlighten us about the incident shown? No names are legible on the ships, but a distant warehouse carries the title 'Jessop & Cie.' There are no other clues to where or when.

43/05. This is a good, clear picture of a paddle steamer, but a piece of timber obscures the point on the paddle box where a name is usually displayed. No publisher is credited and the card has not been posted, so we have no date. Can anyone suggest a name and even a location?

43/06. This boat is named *Curlew* and a caption across the top tells us she was 'built by us last month for the colonies'. Can anyone identify the builder's yard so we can perhaps work out which *Curlew* it was?